redefining
life: **MYPURPOSE**

redefining
life: MYPURPOSE

A NAVSTUDY FEATURING THEMESSAGE®//REMIX™

Written and compiled by Margaret Feinberg

Th1nk Books
an imprint of NavPress®

TH1NK
P.O. Box 35001
Colorado Springs, Colorado 80935

www.navpress.com

TH1NK is an imprint of NavPress.

ISBN 1-57683-827-7

Cover design by Kirk DouPonce, Dog Eared Design
Cover photo by Robert Daly, Getty
Creative Team: Gabe Filkey, s.c.m., Steve Parolini, Arvid Wallen,
                Kathy Mosier, Glynese Northam

Written and compiled by Margaret Feinberg

Printed in Canada

2 3 4 5 6 7 8 9 10 / 09 08 07 06

contents

about the redefininglife series

It's in Christ that we find out who we are and what we are living for.

Ephesians 1:11

For most of your life, you've been a student. And yet in a moment—probably marked by a ceremony—the title you carried for more than a dozen years was stripped away. So now how will you describe yourself when people ask? Are you a professional? An adult? A temporarily unemployed graduate? What seems to fit? Or do any of these fit at all?

Expectations are probably pretty high. But only a few of your graduating class fall into the life you wish you could have—the great job, the wonderful lifelong relationship, the incredible devotion to God. For the rest of you, it's back to square one in many ways. What has been defined for you in the past is suddenly up for negotiation.

The discussion guides in the REDEFINING LIFE series give you a forum to help with that negotiation process. They can help you figure out who you are, *who you really are,* whether you're still taking classes, employed full-time, or somewhere in between. They can help you find out what's really important in life, how to thrive in your work, and how to grow lifelong, meaningful relationships.

REDEFINING LIFE is a place to ask the hard questions of yourself and others. We're talking about a "marrow deep" kind of honesty. At the very least, these discussion guides will show you that you're not alone in the process of self-definition. And hopefully, they will also give you a glimpse—or maybe more—of God's role in the defining of you.

introduction

Your body has many parts—limbs, organs, cells—but no matter how many parts you can name, you're still one body. It's exactly the same with Christ. By means of his one Spirit, we all said goodbye to our partial and piecemeal lives. We each used to independently call our own shots, but then we entered into a large and integrated life in which *he* has the final say in everything. (This is what we proclaimed in word and action when we were baptized.) Each of us is now a part of his resurrection body, refreshed and sustained at one fountain—his Spirit—where we all come to drink. The old labels we once used to identify ourselves—labels like Jew or Greek, slave or free—are no longer useful. We need something larger, more comprehensive.

I want you to think about how all this makes you more significant, not less. A body isn't just a single part blown up into something huge. It's all the different-but-similar parts arranged and functioning together. . . .

But I also want you to think about how this keeps your significance from getting blown up into self-importance. For no matter how significant you are, it is only because of what you are a *part* of. An enormous eye or a gigantic hand wouldn't be a body, but a monster.

1 Corinthians 12:12-14,19

Do you know people who truly believe their life matters? If so, you probably notice that this belief affects everything they do. They can't help but walk a little differently. Maybe this difference comes from a confidence born of skill or schooling or mentoring. Or a clear sense of mission. Or maybe just a greater sense of trust that they're heading in generally the right direction.

One thing is certain: These individuals carry themselves with a sense of significance. They have a grasp, however faint or obvious it might be, of why they're *really* here, and it compels them to live by moving forward rather than languishing in the hamster wheel of a go-nowhere life.

These people raise a deep question for the rest of us: What makes the difference between merely being alive and really living? Could it possibly be a sense of purpose, of calling, of mission that breathes the "extra" into the ordinary? Is it the sense that we are part of a bigger story—of a "large and integrated life"? And if so, how do we get there?

In this discussion guide you are going to be challenged to ask yourself some tough questions about your significance—and where you find it. You may feel a little uncomfortable at times. After all, this kind of soul searching—the kind that can actually help reshape the human spirit—is never safe. But if it presses you toward a new understanding of yourself and God's purpose for your life, then it will be well worth it.

What you won't find here is a carefully annotated Plan for Your Life. Purpose is bigger than plot points on a personal timescale. It's more than your job and bigger even than your relationships. This study is all about getting you to look at the Bigger Purpose. As you examine what that looks like, you'll hopefully discover how to make better daily choices—the kind that *do* end up in a Day-Timer or Palm Pilot.

how to use this discussion guide

REDEFINING LIFE isn't like any other study. We're not kidding. REDEFINING LIFE isn't designed with easy, obvious-to-answer questions and nice fill-in-the-blanks. It's got more of a wide-open-spaces feel to it.

The process is simple, really. Complete a lesson *on your own* (see details below). Then get with your small group and go through it again *together*. Got it?

Okay, want a little more direction than that? Here you go. And if you want even more help, check out the Discussion Group Study Tips (page 135) and the Frequently Asked Questions (page 137) sections in the back of the book.

1. Read, read, read. Each lesson contains five sections, but don't think of them as homework. This isn't an assignment to be graded. And at the end of the week, you don't have to turn it in to a teacher, professor, or boss. So don't read this as a "have to" but as a "get to." Think about how you read when you're on vacation. Set a leisurely pace. Try to enjoy what you read. Then read it again. Allow the words and meaning to

first thoughts
like:
dislike:
agree:
disagree:
don't get it:

soak in. Use the First Thoughts box to record your initial reactions to the text. (That's a sample on the previous page.) Then use the space provided in and around the reading to make notes. What bugs you? What inspires you? What doesn't make sense? What's confusing? Be honest. Be real. Be yourself. Don't shy away from phrases or sentences you don't understand or don't like. Circle them. Cross them out. Add exclamation marks or smiley faces.

2. Think about what you read. Think about what you wrote. Always ask:

- What does this mean?
- Why does this matter?
- How does this relate to my life right now?
- What does Scripture have to say about this?

Then respond to the questions provided. If you have a knack for asking questions, don't be shy about writing some of your own. You may have a lot to say on one topic, little on another. That's okay. When you come back to the passages in your small group, listen. Allow the experience of others to broaden your understanding and wisdom. You'll be stretched here—called on to evaluate what you've discovered and asked to make practical sense of it. In community, that stretching can often be painful and sometimes even embarrassing. But your willingness to be transparent—your openness to the possibility of personal growth—will reap great rewards. Vulnerability spurs growth in yourself and others.

3. Pray as you go through the entire session—before you begin reading, as you're thinking about a passage and its questions, and especially before you get together in a small group. Pause 'n' pray whenever you need to ask God for help along the way. Prayer takes many forms. You can speak your prayers. Be silent. Write them in the space at the bottom of each page. You can pray a Scripture or a spiritual song. Just don't forget that one of the most important parts of prayer is taking time to listen for God's response.

4. Live. What good are study, reflection, and prayer if they don't lead to action? When reflecting on the week's worth of lessons, think about what impacted you and how you can turn that lesson into action. After studying the issue of forgiveness, you may realize you need to write a letter or email to someone. After studying God's generosity, you may feel compelled to give a gift to a particular outreach. Figure out what God is calling you to do to live out your faith. Sometimes you'll finish a week's worth of lessons and each group member will decide to commit to the same goal. Other times you'll each walk away with a different conviction or goal. Record your goals in the book.

5. Follow up. What good are information and conversation if they don't lead to transformation? Your goal in doing any good study is to ultimately become more like Christ, and this is no exception. Prepare yourself to take your faith and make it active and alive. Be willing to set goals and hold others (as well as be held) accountable in your group. Part of being in a community of Jesus-followers means asking, "Hey, did you do what you said you were going to do?" It will help you put your faith into action as part of a community.

6. Repeat as necessary.

the
compelling

God, your God, is above all a compassionate God. In the end he will not abandon you, he won't bring you to ruin, he won't forget the covenant with your ancestors which he swore to them. Ask questions. Find out what has been going on all these years before you were born.

Deuteronomy 4:31-32

the defining line

We start every lesson by asking you to do a sometimes-difficult thing: define the core truths about the study topic as it relates to you right now. Use this "beginning place" to set the foundation for the lesson. You can then build, change, adjust, and otherwise redefine your life from here.

You can travel along a set of train tracks for a long time without knowing much about the journey. You may be able to tell someone the place where you started, and you can read the destination off your ticket stub. But there's no guarantee that you'll be able to tell someone much about the train itself or the wonder of travel.

How about your life journey? You know the beginning (it's likely chronicled in embarrassing baby pictures), and the ending is the same for everyone: death. But the wonder of it . . . do you know that? Can you articulate the experience of this life path you're traveling? Do you know what cities you'll pass through—where the tracks will take you before that ultimate destination?

Think for a moment about why you're engaged in this study. What compelled you to pick up this book? Why were you willing to join with other spiritual pilgrims? Record your answers.

Now dig a little deeper. What motivates you to grow in your life and in your faith? What compels you to go to work or class every day? What gets you out of bed? Use the space below to describe what really drives you to move forward.

Consider sharing your responses with your group when you meet.

read The Buy-In

Genesis 3:1-5

The serpent was clever, more clever than any wild animal GOD had made. He spoke to the Woman: "Do I understand that God told you not to eat from any tree in the garden?"

The Woman said to the serpent, "Not at all. We can eat from the trees in the garden. It's only about the tree in the middle of the garden that God said, 'Don't eat from it; don't even touch it or you'll die.'"

The serpent told the Woman, "You won't die. God knows that the moment you eat from that tree, you'll see what's really going on. You'll be just like God, knowing everything, ranging all the way from good to evil."

---

first thoughts

like:

dislike:

agree:

disagree:

don't get it:

---

think

- Why do you think the serpent's words were so enticing to Eve? Do you think they're still enticing today?
- Would you be tempted to "see what's really going on"? Why or why not?
- What prompts people (include yourself here) to want to know God's plans? Do you think you'd live life differently if you knew God's plans for you? Or is the discovery of those plans part of the plan itself?
- In what ways do you battle the desire to be like God?

pray

read Building Purpose Apart from God

Genesis 11:2-8

It so happened that as they moved out of the east, they came upon a plain in the land of Shinar and settled down.

They said to one another, "Come, let's make bricks and fire them well." They used brick for stone and tar for mortar.

Then they said, "Come, let's build ourselves a city and a tower that reaches Heaven. Let's make ourselves famous so we won't be scattered here and there across the Earth."

GOD came down to look over the city and the tower those people had built.

GOD took one look and said, "One people, one language; why, this is only a first step. No telling what they'll come up with next—they'll stop at nothing! Come, we'll go down and garble their speech so they won't understand each other." Then GOD scattered them from there all over the world. And they had to quit building the city.

---

first thoughts

like:

dislike:

agree:

disagree:

don't get it:

---

think

- What does this passage suggest happens when people try to find their purpose apart from God?
- Why do you think there is a tendency for humans to develop a purpose that doesn't involve God? In what ways do you wrestle with this tendency?
- Where do you find your purpose most easily? Is this something you'd like to change? Explain.
- Why do you think it's so easy for people to find their purpose in their work?
- How do you separate your work from your value and purpose?

pray

read Compelling Love

From "Finding Yourself in 'Love'" by Myles Werntz[1]

Over the course of that year, I fell for a girl that was too hot for Texas itself. I wrote short, pithy emails that waxed eloquently about my life and what I was thinking and reading, and too little about things that made any difference. I forgot my friends. I did a lot of dumb things that, four years later, I try to remember with any sense of dignity.

Like falling in love. . . .

In retrospect, I wish I could say that I had listened to the still small voice that was saying in no uncertain terms, "THIS IS A REALLY BAD IDEA." Not bad on the level of putting our car into reverse in mid-traffic—more bad along the lines of attaching my hungry little heart to situations I knew would never answer my yearnings. Always obey these little impulses; they're more than retrograde evolutionary leftovers—they are the pinprick of God, the still small voice and the fire in the bush. Ignore them at your own risk.

As Augustine points out, we do a lot of things for love, stupid and otherwise. But isn't it just like God, Augustine says, to use the one thing we cherish, the one thing that burns us like terror, to draw us to God. We pursue and are pursued by God, out of love. We do it for love.

In his *Confessions*, Augustine reveals something very simple about this whole matter that levels my silliness about love: that, at the same time it is readily available, it is also the hardest thing to come by in all creation. Above all desires of the human heart, love renders us unable to speak about anything and everything. It levels the male verbally illiterate, a sponge with legs. From birth, we crawl towards it, toddle towards it, walk, run, stride, and hobble towards the one force in the universe that God compels all creation to respond by: love.

But here's the trick: love, when it's real, is hot as summer asphalt. It makes no promise to coddle or always reaffirm us. Rather, it makes the solemn oath to never leave and to burn the hell out of us—to make us real, to leave us without illusions about ourselves or the world.

In all their glory, all other forces in life are nothing more than the heat without the fire. They are the reflection of the sun off of the windowpane, inviting us to stick our dirty paws up to the glass, warming our hands, but come sundown, leaving us cold and wanting. And like dogs, we keep forgetting the trick and coming back every day, hoping that maybe this will be the day that the glass will be warmer, maybe warm enough to hold onto the heat through the night. But love, love burns bright enough to compel us, but hot enough to keep us humble, drawn to it in awe, but humbled by its magnitude. It makes no offers of safety; in fact, it offers to level us to the ground.

---

first thoughts

like:

dislike:

agree:

disagree:

don't get it:

---

think

- Respond to this quote: "Love burns bright enough to compel us, but hot enough to keep us humble."
- Why do people crave love? What do you think drives that craving? What role does God have in this human craving for love?
- List three crazy things love has compelled you to do. (Share at least one with the group.)
- How are loving and being loved tied into your purpose? How do they shape your decisions?

pray

read Love Actually

From *You Didn't Complete Me: When "the One" Turns Out to Be Just Someone* by JoAnna Harris[2]

Singles Bible studies are always the same it seems—full of sideways glances and awkward introductions. Everyone acting as if they are there to study God's Word, not to meet someone interesting. And maybe it's both. We were told to cluster into groups of five and answer an age-old question: What drives you? Lots of people jumped to say money, and I agreed. Some said power. Career. Fame. After further discussion, we decided there's one main thing that drives us. Acceptance. We want money to be rich to be accepted. We want power to gain respect to gain acceptance. We want fame to be known to be accepted. We want to be prettier or thinner to be accepted. To be loved. And maybe that's the root of it all. We want to be loved.

When you have a boyfriend or a husband, strangers know that someone loves you. You don't have to prove to anyone that you are lovable because it's evident when you arrive at parties as part of a pair. Everyone knows. The movie ticket seller knows. The waiter knows. Your coworkers know. Someone loves you. You have been accepted. And if you don't have some visible badge of acceptance, people simply ask, trying to figure out if you're okay. How's your love life? Do you have a girlfriend? Are you dating anyone? Is there anyone special in your life? If you say no, people either feel sorry for you or look you up and down wondering what you should fix. And it doesn't end if you are actually dating someone. Then there's, When are you getting engaged? When's the

---

first thoughts

like:

dislike:

agree:

disagree:

don't get it:

---

wedding? When do you think he'll ask? Do you think she'll say yes? I don't know about you, but these statements can tend to sound like, Does anyone love you? Are you acceptable? Are you worth anything?

think

- What drives you? Do you agree with Harris that acceptance is the core issue, or do you think there is something more?
- Whether or not you are married, consider this question: What impact do you think marriage has on purpose? In what ways does a person's purpose change in marriage? In what ways does it stay the same? How does that affect how you're living now?
- How does feeling accepted impact the decisions you make in life? At work? Among friends? With family? With God?
- Do you ever wrestle with God's acceptance of you? How so?

pray

read A Purpose for Everything?

2 Corinthians 7:5-11

When we arrived in Macedonia province, we couldn't settle down. The fights in the church and the fears in our hearts kept us on pins and needles. We couldn't relax because we didn't know how it would turn out. Then the God who lifts up the downcast lifted our heads and our hearts with the arrival of Titus. We were glad just to see him, but the true reassurance came in what he told us about you: how much you cared, how much you grieved, how concerned you were for me. I went from worry to tranquility in no time!

I know I distressed you greatly with my letter. Although I felt awful at the time, I don't feel at all bad now that I see how it turned out. The letter upset you, but only for a while. Now I'm glad—not that you were upset, but that you were jarred into turning things around. You let the distress bring you to God, not drive you from him. The result was all gain, no loss.

Distress that drives us to God does that. It turns us around. It gets us back in the way of salvation. We never regret that kind of pain. But those who let distress drive them away from God are full of regrets, end up on a deathbed of regrets.

And now, isn't it wonderful all the ways in which this distress has goaded you closer to God? You're more alive, more concerned, more sensitive, more reverent, more human, more passionate, more responsible. Looked at from any angle, you've come out of this with purity of heart.

---

first thoughts

like:

dislike:

agree:

disagree:

don't get it:

---

think

- The passage says, "Distress that drives us to God does that. It turns us around." In what ways has distress brought you closer to God? In what ways has it taken you further away from Him?
- Do you think everything has a purpose? Explain.
- In your experience, what purpose does pain have? How can pain have a redemptive purpose?
- How does pain — or an aversion to pain — motivate you?

pray

live   The Redefining

Take a few moments to skim through the notes you've made in these readings. What do they tell you about the things that compel you, that define your purpose? Based on what you've read and discussed, is there anything you want to change? Describe this below.

What, if anything, is stopping you from making this change?

Why is knowing your purpose so important? Where are you in the journey of knowing your purpose? Is your purpose tangible? Is it something you're still trying to discover? Do you find yourself wrestling with your purpose indirectly through other circumstances and decisions? Explain.

In the space below, write a statement of your purpose as you understand it. Remember that it's just a rough draft.

Talk with a close friend about all of the above. Brainstorm together about what it might take to move toward God in this area of your life. Determine what this looks like in a practical sense and then list any measurable goals you want to shoot for here. Review these goals each week to see how you're doing.

just like
Christ

What marvelous love the Father has extended to us!
Just look at it—we're called children of God! That's
who we really are. But that's also why the world
doesn't recognize us or take us seriously, because
it has no idea who he is or what he's up to.

   But friends, that's exactly who we are: children of God. And that's only the beginning. Who
knows how we'll end up! What we know is that when
Christ is openly revealed, we'll see him—and in
seeing him, become like him.

1 John 3:1-2

a reminder

*Before you dive into this study, spend a little time reviewing what
you wrote in the previous lesson's Live section. How are you doing?
Check with your small-group members and review your progress
toward the specified goals. If necessary, adjust your goals and plans
and then recommit to them.*

the defining line

The Bible makes it clear that one of our main purposes is to become like
Christ—yet it's also one of the most challenging prospects. In becoming
like Christ, we are forced to let go of our self-serving nature and embrace
God's nature, which is both holy and pure. The idea of becoming like Christ

sets us in pursuit of transformation. It invites us to become what we are truly meant to be. How has your relationship with Christ impacted you? How has it shaped your thought patterns and reactions?

Describe some of the specific ways that being a Christ-follower affects your behavior.

In what ways has being a Christian made you a better person? Are there any ways in which being a Christian has had adverse effects on you?

Consider sharing your responses with your group when you meet.

read The Original Design

Genesis 1:26-28

God spoke: "Let us make human beings in our image, make them
    reflecting our nature
So they can be responsible for the fish in the sea,
    the birds in the air, the cattle,
And, yes, Earth itself,
    and every animal that moves on the face of Earth."
God created human beings;
    he created them godlike,
Reflecting God's nature.
    He created them male and female.
God blessed them:
    "Prosper! Reproduce! Fill Earth! Take charge!
Be responsible for fish in the sea and birds in the air,
    for every living thing that moves on the face of Earth."

Genesis 2:4-7

This is the story of how it all started,
    of Heaven and Earth when they were created.

At the time GOD made Earth and Heaven, before any grasses or shrubs had
sprouted from the ground—GOD hadn't yet sent rain on Earth, nor was
there anyone around to work the ground (the whole Earth was watered by
underground springs)—GOD formed Man out of dirt from the ground and
blew into his nostrils the breath of life. The Man came alive—a living soul!

first thoughts

like:

dislike:

agree:

disagree:

don't get it:

think

- What do these passages reveal about God's original design for humanity? What do they reveal about our original purpose?
- How far has mankind drifted from what is described in these passages? In what ways are we still tracking with what's described?
- Why is it important to know the roots of humanity? What do they reveal about us today?
- In what ways do you reflect your Creator? In what ways is the reflection murky?
- Describe a moment in your own life when you felt a bit of the harmony between God and mankind described in these passages. How do you reconcile your answers to the previous two questions?

pray

read Inside Out

Romans 12:1-13

So here's what I want you to do, God helping you: Take your everyday, ordinary life—your sleeping, eating, going-to-work, and walking-around life—and place it before God as an offering. Embracing what God does for you is the best thing you can do for him. Don't become so well-adjusted to your culture that you fit into it without even thinking. Instead, fix your attention on God. You'll be changed from the inside out. Readily recognize what he wants from you, and quickly respond to it. Unlike the culture around you, always dragging you down to its level of immaturity, God brings the best out of you, develops well-formed maturity in you.

I'm speaking to you out of deep gratitude for all that God has given me, and especially as I have responsibilities in relation to you. Living then, as every one of you does, in pure grace, it's important that you not misinterpret yourselves as people who are bringing this goodness to God. No, God brings it all to you. The only accurate way to understand ourselves is by what God is and by what he does for us, not by what we are and what we do for him.

In this way we are like the various parts of a human body. Each part gets its meaning from the body as a whole, not the other way around. The body we're talking about is Christ's body of chosen people. Each of us finds our meaning and function as a part of his body. But as a chopped-off finger or cut-off toe we wouldn't amount to much, would we? So since we find ourselves fashioned into all these excellently formed and marvelously functioning parts in Christ's body, let's just go ahead and be what we were made to be, without enviously or pridefully comparing ourselves with each other, or trying to be something we aren't.

If you preach, just preach God's Message, nothing else; if you help, just help, don't take over; if you teach, stick to your teaching; if you give encouraging guidance, be careful that you don't get bossy; if you're put in charge, don't manipulate; if you're called to give aid to people in distress, keep your eyes open and be quick to respond; if you work with the disadvantaged, don't let yourself get irritated with them or depressed by them. Keep a smile on your face.

Love from the center of who you are; don't fake it. Run for dear life from evil; hold on for dear life to good. Be good friends who love deeply; practice playing second fiddle.

Don't burn out; keep yourselves fueled and aflame. Be alert servants of the Master, cheerfully expectant. Don't quit in hard times; pray all the harder. Help needy Christians; be inventive in hospitality.

---

first thoughts

like:

dislike:

agree:

disagree:

don't get it:

---

think

- Is there any aspect of your life that doesn't call for transformation? Explain.
- Prioritize the top three ways or areas in which you feel God is transforming you. In considering your need for transformation, would you have prioritized them the same way God has? Why or why not?
- What does it look like to become like Christ? How does that play into an examination of your purpose?
- Does transformation cost anything? If so, what does it cost? What has it cost you? Are you willing to pay it again?

pray

read Transformation

From "Grace"[1]

The boy stood with back arched, head cocked, back and hands clenched defiantly. "Go ahead, give it to me."

The principal looked down at the young rebel. "How many times have you been here?"

The child sneered rebelliously. "Apparently not enough."

The principal gave the boy a strange look. "And you have been punished each time, have you not?"

"Yeah, I been punished, if that's what you want to call it." He threw out his small chest. "Go ahead, I can take whatever you dish out. I always have."

"And no thought of your punishment enters your head the next time you decide to break the rules, does it?"

"Nope, I do whatever I want to do. Ain't nothin' you people gonna do to stop me, either."

The principal looked over at the teacher who stood nearby. "What did he do this time?"

"Fighting. He took little Tommy and shoved his face into the sandbox."

The principal turned to look at the boy. "Why? What did little Tommy do to you?"

"Nothin'. I didn't like the way he was lookin' at me, just like I don't like the way you're lookin' at me! And if I thought I could do it, I'd shove your face into something."

The teacher stiffened and started to rise but a quick look from the principal stopped him. He contemplated the child for a moment and then quietly said, "Today, my young student, is the day you learn about grace."

"Grace? Isn't that what you old people do before you sit down to eat? I don't need none of your stinkin' grace."

"Oh, but you do." The principal studied the young man's face and whispered, "Oh, yes, you truly do. . . ."

The boy continued to glare as the principal continued, "Grace, in its short definition, is unmerited favor. You cannot earn it; it is a gift and is always freely given. It means that you will not be getting what you so richly deserve."

The boy looked puzzled. "You're not gonna whup me? You just gonna let me walk?"

The principal looked down at the unyielding child. "Yes, I am going to let you walk."

The boy studied the face of the principal. "No punishment at all? Even though I socked Tommy and shoved his face into the sandbox?"

"Oh, there has to be punishment. What you did was wrong and there are always consequences to our actions. There will be punishment. Grace is not an excuse for doing wrong."

"I knew it," sneered the boy as he held out his hands. "Let's get on with it."

The principal nodded toward the teacher. "Bring me the paddle." The teacher presented the paddle to the principal. He looked at it and then handed it back to the teacher. He looked at the child and said, "I want you to count the blows." He slid out from behind his desk and walked over to stand directly in front of the young man. He gently reached out and folded the child's outstretched, expectant hands together and then turned to face the teacher with his own hands outstretched. One quiet word came forth from his mouth: "Begin."

The paddle whipped down on the outstretched hands of the principal. Crack!

The young man jumped ten feet in the air. Shock registered across his face. "One," he whispered.

Crack! "Two." His voice raised an octave.

Crack! "Three . . ." He couldn't believe this.

Crack! "Four." Big tears welled up in the eyes of the rebel. "Okay, stop! That's enough. Stop!"

Crack! came the paddle down on the callused hands of the principal.

Crack! The child flinched with each blow, tears beginning to stream down his face.

Crack!

Crack! "No, please," the former rebel begged. "Stop. I did it. I'm the one who deserves it. Stop! Please. Stop . . ." Still the blows came. Crack! Crack! One after another.

Finally it was over. The principal stood with sweat glistening across his forehead and beads trickling down his face. Slowly he knelt down. He studied the young man for a second and then his swollen hands reached out to cradle the face of the weeping child.

"Grace . . ."

---

first thoughts

like:

dislike:

agree:

disagree:

don't get it:

---

think

- What was your immediate reaction to this story? Why do you think you responded in this way?
- What was the transformation that occurred in this young child's life?
- Reflect on a moment of transformation in your own life. What did it look like? What was the cause? What was the effect?
- What role does grace play in becoming like Christ? What role has it played in your personal transformation?
- Do you think God uses a "whupping" as a first or a last resort? Why is it needed at all?

pray

read Deep-Spirited Friends

Philippians 2:1-11

If you've gotten anything at all out of following Christ, if his love has made any difference in your life, if being in a community of the Spirit means anything to you, if you have a heart, if you *care*—then do me a favor: Agree with each other, love each other, be deep-spirited friends. Don't push your way to the front; don't sweet-talk your way to the top. Put yourself aside, and help others get ahead. Don't be obsessed with getting your own advantage. Forget yourselves long enough to lend a helping hand.

Think of yourselves the way Christ Jesus thought of himself. He had equal status with God but didn't think so much of himself that he had to cling to the advantages of that status no matter what. Not at all. When the time came, he set aside the privileges of deity and took on the status of a slave, became *human!* Having become human, he stayed human. It was an incredibly humbling process. He didn't claim special privileges. Instead, he lived a selfless, obedient life and then died a selfless, obedient death—and the worst kind of death at that: a crucifixion.

Because of that obedience, God lifted him high and honored him far beyond anyone or anything, ever, so that all created beings in heaven and on earth—even those long ago dead and buried—will bow in worship before this Jesus Christ, and call out in praise that he is the Master of all, to the glorious honor of God the Father.

---

first thoughts

like:

dislike:

agree:

disagree:

don't get it:

---

think

- Can transformation take place apart from community? What role does community play in transformation?
- Have you ever been part of a real community? What did it look like? How did it impact or transform you?
- What are the greatest benefits of experiencing real community? What are the greatest challenges?
- How can community impact the way in which you learn to become like Christ?

pray

read More to Life

From an anonymous article on www.changedlives.com

For the first 49 years of my life, I chose to ignore God. This was easy for me to do because as a Jewish, atheistic psychologist/college professor who spent most of his life in a liberal educational system, I was among people who believed that a belief in God was just one of many "alternative lifestyles" one could sample from the smorgasbord of life. Quite ironically, my wife was a "born again" Christian and the butt of many of my friends' jokes, much to my embarrassment. People, including myself, considered her a fanatic. In fact, our religious differences almost led to a divorce early in our marriage, which was heartbreaking, as we really loved one another. We even had a divorce date set and it was only by God's intervention that I did not divorce her. Faithfully, she and others prayed for me for 23 years. I stubbornly resisted, resorting to clever theological and scientific arguments—which a major part of our society and educational system taught me—to run from God.

About three years ago, a series of events led me to the belief that there was much more to life than our society had to offer. Although I had a successful career, many friends, financial success, and a wonderful family, I felt much was lacking. Accompanying this was a growing belief that our culture and society was "using me" and telling me lies (such as one must have money and possessions to be happy, for example). I was at the end of my rope, which by the way was exactly where God wanted me. For the first time I prayed in earnest. The first thing I prayed for was for God to remove the wedge that was between my wife and myself. God answered, "What about the wedge that you put between me and you?" I was frozen in awe and revelation; God had spoken to me! There was no way that could have come from my own mind, because 10 minutes before that I was a "dyed in the wool" atheist. I went through a week of dramatic, wonderful and sometimes painful transformation and accepted Jesus Christ as my Lord and Savior. He began to show me a spiritual world that had been in front of my eyes all along but which I was blind to. Sermons and Bible verses which used to seem boring and hackneyed statements of the obvious exploded in my heart; I had found the Truth, that "something special" which I knew life must contain but could not find. Since that wonderful and sweet time, God has blessed me and multiplied my prosperity and filled it with all the good things life should contain. He still speaks to me, answering my prayers, lifting me up and sharing with me His wonders of creation. My cup runneth over. Hallelujah!

---

first thoughts

like:

dislike:

agree:

disagree:

don't get it:

---

think

- Think back on when you became a Christian. What was your conversion experience like? How does it compare to others' experiences?
- People get to know God in a variety of ways. What does this tell you about how God reaches out to people?
- Is there a connection between how you became a Christian and the trajectory that you have been placed on in life? Explain.

pray

live   The Redefining

Take a few moments to skim through the notes you've made in these readings. What do they tell you about becoming like Christ? Based on what you've read and discussed, is there anything you want to change? Describe this below.

What, if anything, is stopping you from making this change?

Make a list of the top five things that drive you. What role does Christ play in each of those areas? How does He respond or want to respond to each of those areas in your life?

What aspects of the transformation to Christlikeness are most difficult for you to grasp? How do you see yourself being transformed?

Talk with a close friend about all of the above. Brainstorm together about what it might take to move toward God in this area of your life. Determine what this looks like in a practical sense and then list any measurable goals you want to shoot for here. Review these goals each week to see how you're doing.

totally
stumped

What I want to talk about now is the various ways God's Spirit gets worked into our lives. This is complex and often misunderstood, but I want you to be informed and knowledgeable. Remember how you were when you didn't know God, led from one phony god to another, never knowing what you were doing, just doing it because everybody else did it? It's different in this life. God wants us to use our intelligence, to seek to understand as well as we can. For instance, by using your heads, you know perfectly well that the Spirit of God would never prompt anyone to say "Jesus be damned!" Nor would anyone be inclined to say "Jesus is Master!" without the insight of the Holy Spirit.

1 Corinthians 12:1-3

a reminder

Before you dive into this study, spend a little time reviewing what you wrote in the previous lessons' Live sections. How are you doing? Check with your small-group members and review your progress toward the specified goals. If necessary, adjust your goals and plans and then recommit to them.

the defining line

God works Himself into the very fabric of creation—including our lives—through countless ways. Yet sometimes knowing God's will proves to be a mystery. Make a list of key moments in your life when God's will was crystal clear to you.

Can you think of a time (or two) when God's will was less clear? Record a few of those moments.

Do you think God's will and His purposes for your life are intended to be crystal clear? Why or why not? How does this issue affect your relationship with God?

Consider sharing your responses with your group when you meet.

read Beyond Understanding

**From *Joni Eareckson: Victory Through Suffering* by
Joni Eareckson Tada**[1]

One hot July afternoon in 1967, I dove into a shallow lake and my life changed forever. I suffered a spinal cord fracture that left me paralyzed from the neck down, without use of my hands and legs. Lying in my hospital bed, I tried desperately to make sense of the horrible turn of events. I begged friends to assist me in suicide. Slit my wrists, dump pills down my throat, anything to end my misery!

And questions! I had so many. I believed in God, but I was angry with Him. If God is supposed to be all-loving and all-powerful, then how could what happened be a demonstration of His love and power? Surely He could have stopped it from happening. How can permanent, lifelong paralysis be a part of His loving plan for me? Unless I found answers, I didn't see how this God could be worthy of my trust.

Steve, a friend of mine, took on my questions. He pointed me to Christ. "Joni, whose will was the cross?" he asked. All those good Sunday School lessons spun through my head and I answered, "God's will, of course."

Yet he showed me how the devil entered into Judas to betray Jesus, how the devil incited the mob and inspired Pilate to hand down mock justice. Heaven and hell had participated in the exact same event that day, each for its own reasons.

But because God aborts devilish schemes to accomplish His own ends, the world's worst murder became the world's only salvation. Through the cross, the floodgates of heaven opened wide for all. That's why we wear this curious emblem of execution around our necks. Jesus changed its meaning. No longer a symbol of death, it has become a symbol of hope and victory.

Steve helped me see that heaven and hell participated in my accident, too. When I took the reckless dive that made me a quadriplegic, the devil probably thought, I have shipwrecked this girl's faith and dashed all her dreams. But God's purpose was probably to turn a stubborn kid into a woman who would reflect patience, endurance and a lively, optimistic hope of heavenly glories above.

In this intensely personal tug-of-war, who gets the glory and whose motive is brought to fulfillment is entirely my choice. For example, my wheelchair used to symbolize for me alienation and confinement. But God has exchanged its meaning because I've trusted in Him. Today this wheelchair symbolizes my independence. It's a choice I made, and one that anyone can make.

I wouldn't dare list 16 biblical reasons why this accident happened to me. But in the 34 years since it happened, I have discovered many good things that have come from my disability. I used to think happiness was a Friday night date, a size 12 dress, and a future with Ethan Allen furniture and 2.5 children. Today I know better. What matters is love: warm, deep, real, personal love with a neighbor, a husband, a sister, an aunt, a nurse or an attendant. It's people who count.

And I live with the heightened awareness that even better things are coming. The good things in this life are only a foreshadowing of more glorious, grand things ready to burst on the scene when we walk into the other side of eternity.

---

first thoughts

like:

dislike:

agree:

disagree:

don't get it:

---

think

- What are your initial reactions to Joni's story? How do you find God's purpose in circumstances that seem so tragic?
- Has God's will ever stumped you? How did you feel? How did you respond? Did His will become clearer later on?
- How does God lead and instruct you? How do you know that God is behind a set of events or circumstances you don't understand?
- Where do God's will and purpose intertwine? Are they separate issues or the same issue for you?

pray

read Beyond Questions

Job 42:1-6

Job answered GOD:
"I'm convinced: You can do anything and everything.
    Nothing and no one can upset your plans.
You asked, 'Who is this muddying the water,
    ignorantly confusing the issue, second-guessing my
        purposes?'
I admit it. I was the one. I babbled on about things far
        beyond me,
    made small talk about wonders way over my head.
You told me, 'Listen, and let me do the talking.
    Let me ask the questions. *You* give the answers.'
I admit I once lived by rumors of you;
    now I have it all firsthand—from my own eyes and ears!
I'm sorry—forgive me. I'll never do that again, I promise!
    I'll never again live on crusts of hearsay, crumbs of rumor."

---

first thoughts

like:

dislike:

agree:

disagree:

don't get it:

---

think

- Have you ever come to a crossroad in life where you had no idea what God's purpose was? What did you do? Looking back, how did you handle the situation? How did God handle it?
- What are the "crusts of hearsay, crumbs of rumor" that sometimes get in your way of hearing God's true purpose?
- Why do you think it's so hard to know God's will? What makes it so confusing?
- Have you ever felt confident that you were following God's will and then found yourself second-guessing your decision? How did you respond? How did you recover? What did you learn?

pray

read Unwavering Obedience

Daniel 1:3-21

The king told Ashpenaz, head of the palace staff, to get some Israelites from the royal family and nobility—young men who were healthy and handsome, intelligent and well-educated, good prospects for leadership positions in the government, perfect specimens!—and indoctrinate them in the Babylonian language and the lore of magic and fortunetelling. The king then ordered that they be served from the same menu as the royal table—the best food, the finest wine. After three years of training they would be given positions in the king's court.

Four young men from Judah—Daniel, Hananiah, Mishael, and Azariah—were among those selected. The head of the palace staff gave them Babylonian names: Daniel was named Belteshazzar, Hananiah was named Shadrach, Mishael was named Meshach, Azariah was named Abednego.

But Daniel determined that he would not defile himself by eating the king's food or drinking his wine, so he asked the head of the palace staff to exempt him from the royal diet. The head of the palace staff, by God's grace, liked Daniel, but he warned him, "I'm afraid of what my master the king will do. He is the one who assigned this diet and if he sees that you are not as healthy as the rest, he'll have my head!"

But Daniel appealed to a steward who had been assigned by the head of the palace staff to be in charge of Daniel, Hananiah, Mishael, and Azariah: "Try us out for ten days on a simple diet of vegetables and water. Then compare us with the young men who eat from the royal menu. Make your decision on the basis of what you see."

The steward agreed to do it and fed them vegetables and water for ten days. At the end of the ten days they looked better and more robust than all the others who had been eating from the royal menu. So the steward continued to exempt them from the royal menu of food and drink and served them only vegetables.

God gave these four young men knowledge and skill in both books and life. In addition, Daniel was gifted in understanding all sorts of visions and dreams. At the end of the time set by the king for their training, the head of the royal staff brought them in to Nebuchadnezzar. When the king interviewed them, he found them far superior to all the other young men. None were a match for Daniel, Hananiah, Mishael, and Azariah.

And so they took their place in the king's service. Whenever the king consulted them on anything, on books or on life, he found them ten times better than all the magicians and enchanters in his kingdom put together.

Daniel continued in the king's service until the first year in the reign of King Cyrus.

first thoughts

like:

dislike:

agree:

disagree:

don't get it:

think

- What intrigues you the most about this story? What role does obedience play in this scenario?
- How important is obedience in responding to God's will? Explain.
- Do you think disobedience can disqualify you from fulfilling God's purposes? Why or why not?
- In what ways are you challenged to live like Daniel in your current situation—your workplace, church, or among your friends?

pray

read The God Whisperer

From *God Whispers: Learning to Hear His Voice* by Margaret Feinberg[2]

God is big. He could use anything to communicate with His people. Think about it. He could fill the sky with a Star Wars presentation, leaving messages beaming in the atmosphere for hours. He could paint His words in nature using everything from tree bark to blooming flowers to freshly fallen snow. He could even use smoke signals or drop parchment from the sky. In modern times, He could send an email, call someone's cell or leave a voice mail message.

But He doesn't.

He takes a much more subtle approach.

Instead of shouting, He whispers.

---

first thoughts

like:

dislike:

agree:

disagree:

don't get it:

---

think

- Why do you think God uses quiet means to get our attention? Wouldn't you rather hear Him shout or communicate by email?
- How loud does God get when He speaks to you?

- What are the different ways God speaks to you? What method does He use most often to reveal Himself to you?
- What do you need to do to hear God? What practical steps do you need to take to make time (and space) to listen to His voice?
- What stops you from taking more time to listen to God's voice and leading in your life?

pray

read The Ultimate Friendship

John 15:14-17

"You are my friends when you do the things I command you. I'm no longer calling you servants because servants don't understand what their master is thinking and planning. No, I've named you friends because I've let you in on everything I've heard from the Father.

"You didn't choose me, remember; I chose you, and put you in the world to bear fruit, fruit that won't spoil. As fruit bearers, whatever you ask the Father in relation to me, he gives you.

"But remember the root command: Love one another."

first thoughts

like:

dislike:

agree:

disagree:

don't get it:

think

- What role can friends play in helping you to discover God's will?
- Do you tilt the scales toward having a public or private personality? How much of yourself do you reveal to your friends? How much of yourself do you reveal to strangers? How might revealing yourself more to friends help in uncovering your purpose?
- Do you think God is more likely to reveal more of His will and Himself to someone who seeks Him? Why or why not?

pray

live   The Redefining

Take a few moments to skim through the notes you've made in these readings. What do they tell you about the challenge of discovering God's will? Based on what you've read and discussed, is there anything you want to change? Describe this below.

What, if anything, is stopping you from making this change?

Do you think part of your purpose is to seek God? Why or why not?

How much are you willing to seek God to know His will? What stops you from seeking Him more? Make a list of three things you are going to do this week to seek God.

Talk with a close friend about all of the above. Brainstorm together about what it might take to move toward God in this area of your life. Determine what this looks like in a practical sense and then list any measurable goals you want to shoot for here. Review these goals each week to see how you're doing.

shouting
stones

They brought the colt to Jesus. Then, throwing their coats on its back, they helped Jesus get on. As he rode, the people gave him a grand welcome, throwing their coats on the street.
Right at the crest, where Mount Olives begins its descent, the whole crowd of disciples burst into enthusiastic praise over all the mighty works they had witnessed:

Blessed is he who comes,
    the king in God's name!
All's well in heaven!
    Glory in the high places!

Some Pharisees from the crowd told him, "Teacher, get your disciples under control!"
But he said, "If they kept quiet, the stones would do it for them, shouting praise."

Luke 19:35-40

a reminder

Before you dive into this study, spend a little time reviewing what you wrote in the previous lessons' Live sections. How are you doing? Check with your small-group members and review your progress toward the specified goals. If necessary, adjust your goals and plans and then recommit to them.

the defining line

The fabric of creation is designed for worship. It's undeniable: You are created for worship. That is certainly a part of your purpose. Take a few moments and record your most memorable worship experiences below. What made them so special?

While worship can be expressed through music, song, and dance, it also can take countless other forms. In what other ways do you express your worship of God?

Consider sharing your responses with your group when you meet.

read Rediscovering Praise

From *Praise Habit* by David Crowder[1]

We instinctively knew what it was to praise something. It's always been in us. We were created for it. It's part of who we are. As kids, we were fabulous at it. But as adults we become self-conscious and awkward. Something gets lost. I think we do it to each other. At some point, I hold the toy up exultantly and you comment that it looks ridiculous to hold the toy up in such a way. It's not a cool toy like I believed it to be. It is worn and tired, you point out. And we slowly chip away at each other's protective coatings of innocence until one day we wake up and notice we are naked and people are pointing.

Occasionally, I'm watching a movie or reading words in a book or I'm walking down a street in California and the breeze on my skin feels full of water, like my arms are floating in a pool, and I'm inspired to live anew in an innocent rediscovering way I haven't thought of in a long time. Then just as I lean in to take a bite, to suck with all my might at the marrow, to breathe in with as much ferocity as I can muster, I see your eyes and hear your whispers.

first thoughts
like:
dislike:
agree:
disagree:
don't get it:

"That is not polite. Use your silverware. If you don't have any we'll get you some. Please, we beg you. It is barbaric and difficult to watch. We have moved beyond this. Come with us. Please. We are becoming uncomfortable."

think

- What do you think about the statement, "We instinctively knew what it was to praise something"? Was that true for you?
- What did this concept of praise look like to you when you were a child?
- How has that definition changed over the years?
- In what way is praise tied to your purpose? Why do you think that?
- If you have lost the ability to praise, how can you rediscover it? What does it cost you to praise?

pray

read True Worship

John 4:5-26

He came into Sychar, a Samaritan village that bordered the field Jacob had given his son Joseph. Jacob's well was still there. Jesus, worn out by the trip, sat down at the well. It was noon.

A woman, a Samaritan, came to draw water. Jesus said, "Would you give me a drink of water?" (His disciples had gone to the village to buy food for lunch.)

The Samaritan woman, taken aback, asked, "How come you, a Jew, are asking me, a Samaritan woman, for a drink?" (Jews in those days wouldn't be caught dead talking to Samaritans.)

Jesus answered, "If you knew the generosity of God and who I am, you would be asking *me* for a drink, and I would give you fresh, living water."

The woman said, "Sir, you don't even have a bucket to draw with, and this well is deep. So how are you going to get this 'living water'? Are you a better man than our ancestor Jacob, who dug this well and drank from it, he and his sons and livestock, and passed it down to us?"

Jesus said, "Everyone who drinks this water will get thirsty again and again. Anyone who drinks the water I give will never thirst—not ever. The water I give will be an artesian spring within, gushing fountains of endless life."

The woman said, "Sir, give me this water so I won't ever get thirsty, won't ever have to come back to this well again!"

He said, "Go call your husband and then come back."

"I have no husband," she said.

"That's nicely put: 'I have no husband.' You've had five husbands, and the man you're living with now isn't even your husband. You spoke the truth there, sure enough."

"Oh, so you're a prophet! Well, tell me this: Our ancestors worshiped God at this mountain, but you Jews insist that Jerusalem is the only place for worship, right?"

"Believe me, woman, the time is coming when you Samaritans will worship the Father neither here at this mountain nor there in Jerusalem. You worship guessing in the dark; we Jews worship in the clear light of day. God's way of salvation is made available through the Jews. But the time is coming—it has, in fact, come—when what you're called will not matter and where you go to worship will not matter.

"It's who you are and the way you live that count before God. Your worship must engage your spirit in the pursuit of truth. That's the kind of people the Father is out looking for: those who are simply and honestly *themselves* before him in their worship. God is sheer being itself—Spirit. Those who worship him must do it out of their very being, their spirits, their true selves, in adoration."

The woman said, "I don't know about that. I do know that the Messiah is coming. When he arrives, we'll get the whole story."

"I am he," said Jesus. "You don't have to wait any longer or look any further."

---

first thoughts

like:

dislike:

agree:

disagree:

don't get it:

---

think

- Why do you think it's so hard to live a life of worship?
- What circumstances—place, time, or atmosphere—are most conducive for your worship?
- How can worship become a more encompassing part of your life?

pray

read Drinking in All of God

Psalm 42

A white-tailed deer drinks
    from the creek;
I want to drink God,
    deep draughts of God.
I'm thirsty for God-alive.
I wonder, "Will I ever make it—
    arrive and drink in God's presence?"
I'm on a diet of tears—
    tears for breakfast, tears for supper.
All day long
    people knock at my door,
Pestering,
    "Where is this God of yours?"

These are the things I go over and over,
    emptying out the pockets of my life.
I was always at the head of the worshiping crowd,
    right out in front,
Leading them all,
    eager to arrive and worship,
Shouting praises, singing thanksgiving—
    celebrating, all of us, God's feast!

Why are you down in the dumps, dear soul?
    Why are you crying the blues?
Fix my eyes on God—
    soon I'll be praising again.
He puts a smile on my face.
    He's my God.

When my soul is in the dumps, I rehearse
    everything I know of you,
From Jordan depths to Hermon heights,
    including Mount Mizar.
Chaos calls to chaos,
    to the tune of whitewater rapids.
Your breaking surf, your thundering breakers
    crash and crush me.
Then GOD promises to love me all day,
    sing songs all through the night!
    My life is God's prayer.

Sometimes I ask God, my rock-solid God,
    "Why did you let me down?
Why am I walking around in tears,
    harassed by enemies?"
They're out for the kill, these
    tormentors with their obscenities,
Taunting day after day,
    "Where is this God of yours?"

Why are you down in the dumps, dear soul?
    Why are you crying the blues?
Fix my eyes on God—
    soon I'll be praising again.
He puts a smile on my face.
    He's my God.

---

first thoughts

like:

dislike:

agree:

disagree:

don't get it:

---

think

- What moods of worship are expressed in this psalm?
- Which of the moods do you relate to most? Which do you relate to least?
- How do your emotions affect your willingness to worship? Does a lack of desire to worship impact how well you're living out God's purpose? Explain.
- How can you worship even when you don't feel like it?

pray

read Hand-Me-Down Worship

Malachi 1:6-14

"Isn't it true that a son honors his father and a worker his master? So if I'm your Father, where's the honor? If I'm your Master, where's the respect?" GOD-of-the-Angel-Armies is calling you on the carpet: "You priests despise me!

"You say, 'Not so! How do we despise you?'

"By your shoddy, sloppy, defiling worship.

"You ask, 'What do you mean, "defiling"? What's defiling about it?'

"When you say, 'The altar of GOD is not important anymore; worship of GOD is no longer a priority,' that's defiling. And when you offer worthless animals for sacrifices in worship, animals that you're trying to get rid of—blind and sick and crippled animals—isn't that defiling? Try a trick like that with your banker or your senator—how far do you think it will get you?" GOD-of-the-Angel-Armies asks you.

"Get on your knees and pray that I will be gracious to you. You priests have gotten everyone in trouble. With this kind of conduct, do you think I'll pay attention to you?" GOD-of-the-Angel-Armies asks you.

"Why doesn't one of you just shut the Temple doors and lock them? Then none of you can get in and play at religion with this silly, empty-headed worship. I am not pleased. The GOD-of-the-Angel-Armies is not pleased. And I don't want any more of this so-called worship!

"I am honored all over the world. And there are people who know how to worship me all over the world, who honor me by bringing their best to me. They're saying it everywhere: 'God is greater, this GOD-of-the-Angel-Armies.'

"All except you. Instead of honoring me, you profane me. You profane me when you say, 'Worship is not important, and what we bring to worship is of no account,' and when you say, 'I'm bored—this doesn't do anything for me.' You act so superior, sticking your noses in the air—act superior to *me*, GOD-of-the-Angel-Armies! And when you do offer something to me, it's a hand-me-down, or broken, or useless. Do you think I'm going to accept it? This is GOD speaking to you!

"A curse on the person who makes a big show of doing something great for me—an expensive sacrifice, say—and then at the last minute brings in something puny and worthless! I'm a great king, GOD-of-the-Angel-Armies, honored far and wide, and I'll not put up with it!"

---

first thoughts

like:

dislike:

agree:

disagree:

don't get it:

---

think

- Do you ever feel like your worship of God is worthless or shoddy? When?
- How do you relate to God when you don't feel like worshiping?
- What makes worship valuable to God? What does God seek in His worshipers?
- How does worship affect God? How does it affect you?

pray

read The God Center

From "Tim Hughes Interview" by Matt Redman[2]

As a songwriter I've been really challenged to write songs that are totally God-centered. Songs that speak of the mystery and the glory of the One we love. It has been a definite conscious decision to try and write these types of worship songs. I love the passage in Revelation 5 — a picture of the worship that surrounds the throne. It's all centered around Christ — the Lamb that was slain. We then see the four living creatures and the twenty-four elders offering up songs of praise. As we move on we glimpse many angels, thousands upon thousands, ten thousand times ten thousand, caught up in worship. You start to wonder, where do we fit in to all of this? Well here you go, "Then I heard every creature in heaven and earth and under the earth and on the sea, and all that is in them singing: 'To Him who sits on the throne and to the Lamb be praise and honour and glory and power, for ever and ever'" (Rev. 5:13). We're included with all the animals — the donkeys, the flies, the swans, and the goldfish. Our worship has to be about God; it can't be centered on ourselves. Practically as I've tried to immerse myself in Scripture these themes have poured out. Also creation I think speaks wonderfully of the beauty and greatness of God. His mighty works are displayed all around us — an amazing sunset, the wonder of new life. His glory echoes all around the world. We need to write more of these types of songs. . . .

I've been thinking a lot about the link between worship and lament. I guess it came at a time when my head was spinning with questions. Life contains so much joy, but along with this, so much pain. I was finding a few things in my life very hard. One night I was in a hotel room in Canada, feeling really low. I sat down to worship and to try and express all that was going on in my mind. The words, "I've had questions, without answers. I've known sorrow. I have known pain," poured out of me. It all felt quite bleak. I started to think though, when you make a statement like that, how do you follow it up? For me as a believer it was to look to Jesus. "But there is one thing, that I'll cling to. You are faithful, Jesus You're true." It was funny as I worshipped out of my brokenness, and the reality of all that was going on, I really met with God. I didn't want to sing "Dance," or "The Happy Song." I wanted to be real. I kept working on the song, but initially thought that it wouldn't be appropriate for a congregation. We don't sing many songs of lament in church. However as I read through Scripture, especially the Psalms, I realized that pain is so freely expressed. "How long O Lord? Will you forget me forever? How long must I wrestle with my thoughts and every day have sorrow in my heart?" (Ps. 13) There has to be a place for honesty and brokenness. However as we read through these Scriptures, the heartfelt cry is turned to worship. Following on from these verses in Psalm 13, "But I will trust in your unfailing love; my heart rejoices in your salvation. I will sing to the Lord for he has been good to me." Amazing. For me that is an incredible statement of faith. When life is falling apart around you, when loved ones die, when sickness is upon you—in that place do you have faith to say, "You are good"? For me I've been trying to write songs that are honest and real. I feel strongly that there has to be a place for these types of songs in our church services.

---

first thoughts

like:

dislike:

agree:

disagree:

don't get it:

---

think

- How freely can you express yourself to God in worship?
- Do you leave time and room for songs of lament in your life? What do they sound like?
- What can you do to make your worship more God-centered?
- What are some ways that you fulfill your purpose through worship?

pray

live   The Redefining

Take a few moments to skim through the notes you've made in these readings. What do they tell you about the role of worship in your life? Based on what you've read and discussed, is there anything you want to change? Describe this below.

What, if anything, is stopping you from making this change?

In the space below, create your own definition of worship based on the Scriptures and passages you've read in this lesson.

How does your life look like this definition? In what ways is your life at odds with this definition? What can you do to make your life more worshipful? Make a list of ideas.

Talk with a close friend about all of the above. Brainstorm together about what it might take to move toward God in this area of your life. Determine what this looks like in a practical sense and then list any measurable goals you want to shoot for here. Review these goals each week to see how you're doing.

can you
enjoy God?

God, mark us with grace
    and blessing! Smile!
The whole country will see how you work,
    all the godless nations see how you save.
God! Let people thank and enjoy you.
    Let all people thank and enjoy you.
Let all far-flung people become happy
    and shout their happiness because
You judge them fair and square,
    you tend the far-flung peoples.
God! Let people thank and enjoy you.
    Let all people thank and enjoy you.
Earth, display your exuberance!
    You mark us with blessing, O God, our God.
You mark us with blessing, O God.
    Earth's four corners—honor him!

Psalm 67

a reminder

Before you dive into this study, spend a little time reviewing what you wrote in the previous lessons' Live sections. How are you doing? Check with your small-group members and review your progress toward the specified goals. If necessary, adjust your goals and plans and then recommit to them.

the defining line

Enjoying God can seem like a strange idea at first glance. God is to be worshiped, feared, and revered. But enjoyed? Scripture makes it clear that we are to enjoy God, but what does that mean? Write your thoughts below.

In what ways does your religious upbringing or understanding of God prevent you from enjoying Him?

How might enjoyment of God fit into your life purpose?

Consider sharing your responses with your group when you meet.

read Partying with God

Nehemiah 8:9-12

Nehemiah the governor, along with Ezra the priest and scholar and the Levites who were teaching the people, said to all the people, "This day is holy to GOD, your God. Don't weep and carry on." They said this because all the people were weeping as they heard the words of The Revelation.

He continued, "Go home and prepare a feast, holiday food and drink; and share it with those who don't have anything: This day is holy to God. Don't feel bad. The joy of GOD is your strength!"

The Levites calmed the people, "Quiet now. This is a holy day. Don't be upset."

So the people went off to feast, eating and drinking and including the poor in a great celebration. Now they got it; they understood the reading that had been given to them.

---

first thoughts

like:

dislike:

agree:

disagree:

don't get it:

---

think

- What place do celebrations and feasts — okay, parties — have in the life of a follower of Christ?
- Do you tend to feel closer to God when you experience tough times or when you experience celebration and joy? Why? How does each reaction make you feel?
- Why did God give us the capacity for joy? What does the phrase "the joy of GOD is your strength" mean to you?
- Describe a few moments in your life when you've truly enjoyed God.
- If part of your life purpose is to enjoy God, how well are you fulfilling this part?

pray

read The Good Thing

Psalm 16:8-11

Day and night I'll stick with GOD;
    I've got a good thing going and I'm not letting go.

I'm happy from the inside out,
    and from the outside in, I'm firmly formed.
You canceled my ticket to hell—
    that's not my destination!

Now you've got my feet on the life path,
    all radiant from the shining of your face.
Ever since you took my hand,
    I'm on the right way.

---

first thoughts

like:

dislike:

agree:

disagree:

don't get it:

---

think

- What good thing do you have going with God? How often do you take time to reflect on God's goodness? What prevents you from doing it more often?
- In what ways do you resonate with the psalmist? In what ways do you disagree or question the psalmist?
- What does God's invitation to enjoy Him look like to you? How often do you accept the invitation?
- How is enjoying God tied into your purpose?

pray

read Intimate and Organic

John 15:4-12

"Live in me. Make your home in me just as I do in you. In the same way that a branch can't bear grapes by itself but only by being joined to the vine, you can't bear fruit unless you are joined with me.

"I am the Vine, you are the branches. When you're joined with me and I with you, the relation intimate and organic, the harvest is sure to be abundant. Separated, you can't produce a thing. Anyone who separates from me is deadwood, gathered up and thrown on the bonfire. But if you make yourselves at home with me and my words are at home in you, you can be sure that whatever you ask will be listened to and acted upon. This is how my Father shows who he is—when you produce grapes, when you mature as my disciples.

"I've loved you the way my Father has loved me. Make yourselves at home in my love. If you keep my commands, you'll remain intimately at home in my love. That's what I've done—kept my Father's commands and made myself at home in his love.

"I've told you these things for a purpose: that my joy might be your joy, and your joy wholly mature. This is my command: Love one another the way I loved you."

---

first thoughts

like:

dislike:

agree:

disagree:

don't get it:

---

think

- What does it mean to you on a personal level to make your home in Christ? What does an "intimate and organic" relationship feel like? What does it look like?
- How does making your home in Christ help you fulfill your calling and purpose?
- To what extent is it possible to fulfill your purpose without this kind of connection with Christ?

pray

read Defying Gravity

From *Orthodoxy* by G. K. Chesterton[1]

A characteristic of the great saints is their power of levity. Angels can fly because they can take themselves lightly. This has been always the instinct of Christendom, and especially the instinct of Christian art. . . . Every figure seems ready to fly up and float about in the heavens. The tattered cloak of the beggar will bear him up like the rayed plumes of the angels. But the kings in their heavy gold and the proud in their robes of purple will all of their nature sink downwards, for pride cannot rise to levity or levitation. Pride is the downward drag of all things into an easy solemnity. One "settles down" into a sort of selfish seriousness; but one has to rise to a gay self-forgetfulness. A man "falls" into a brown study; he reaches up at a blue sky. Seriousness is not a virtue. It would be a heresy, but a much more sensible heresy, to say that seriousness is a vice. It is really a natural trend or lapse into taking one's self gravely, because it is the easiest thing to do. It is much easier to write a *Good Times* leading article than a good joke in *Punch*. For solemnity flows out of men naturally but laughter is a leap. It is easy to be heavy: hard to be light. Satan fell by the force of gravity.

---

first thoughts

like:

dislike:

agree:

disagree:

don't get it:

---

think

- Would you say "laughter is a leap" in your life, or does it come naturally?
- Do you think God has a sense of humor? Why or why not?
- How is God glorified through our laughter and joy?
- What is your response to the idea that God might actually want you to enjoy your life? Is that at odds with anything you've been taught? Do you have enough laughter and lightness in your life? If not, how might you change that?

pray

read The Poverty of a God-Void Life

From "Happiness: Seize the Moment Finding Copper Pennies"[2]

There was a small boy who when walking down the street one day found a bright copper penny. He was so excited that he found money and it didn't cost him anything. This experience led him to spend the rest of his days walking with his head down, eyes wide open, looking for wealth.

During his lifetime he found 1,296,000,000 pennies, 480 nickels, 1,900 dimes, 16,000 quarters, 200 half dollars and thousands of crinkled dollar bills. He accumulated quite a bank account in his lifetime. He prided himself in the fact that he spent his life getting his fortune from nothing.

Yes, the boy, now an old man, spent his life collecting money for nothing. Except that in his lifetime he missed the breathless beauty of 31,369 sunsets, the colorful splendor of 157 rainbows, the fiery beauty of hundreds of maples nipped by autumn's frost. He never saw the thousands of white clouds drifting across blue skies, shifting into various wondrous formations. Birds flying, the sun shining, and the smiles of hundreds of thousands of people that passed through his life. All of this is not a part of his memory. Nor did this man-boy have any time to build a successful family or a circle of true friends. No one cried for him when he passed on; in fact, many were glad to see him leave this world.

---

first thoughts

like:

dislike:

agree:

disagree:

don't get it:

---

think

- Why do you think the coins and crinkled dollar bills had such a grip on the boy? Can you identify anything in your own life that has a similar grip on you?
- Is there anything you may have missed because of your current focus?
- How might your life change if you "looked up" more in your life—if you focused on things that brought happiness or joy?
- How does enjoying God impact your relationship with the world around you or with the people you spend time with?

pray

live   The Redefining

Take a few moments to skim through the notes you've made in these readings. What do they tell you about enjoying the God-life? Based on what you've read and discussed, is there anything you want to change? Describe this below.

What, if anything, is stopping you from making this change?

What are the greatest challenges you anticipate as you seek to enjoy God? Do you ever feel guilty about enjoying things in life? How can you change these feelings in the future?

The enjoyment of God may be a part of your general purpose in life, but what does that mean in everyday practice? How might you enjoy God at work? Among friends? Among strangers? At church?

Talk with a close friend about all of the above. Brainstorm together about what it might take to move toward God in this area of your life. Determine what this looks like in a practical sense and then list any measurable goals you want to shoot for here. Review these goals each week to see how you're doing.

true
community

Don't leave your friends or your parents'
        friends
    and run home to your family when things get
        rough;
Better a nearby friend
    than a distant family.

Proverbs 27:10

a reminder

Before you dive into this study, spend a little time reviewing what you wrote in the previous lessons' Live sections. How are you doing? Check with your small-group members and review your progress toward the specified goals. If necessary, adjust your goals and plans and then recommit to them.

the defining line

There's something to be said for true friends. In fact, there's something wonderful to be said. True friends are able to comfort you, encourage you, and hold you accountable. But they do more than this; they also shape you. In community with others, you learn, you grow, you make slight—or perhaps significant—adjustments. You are shaped.

Make a list of at least three friends who have helped to shape your life over the last few years. Note what kind of impact each person had.

Everyone has a need for authentic community, even the self-proclaimed lone ranger. It may sound trite, but it's true: Everyone needs someone. Reflecting over your life so far, list some things friends and others in your life have done or said that may have shaped or changed you—or redefined your purpose.

Consider sharing your responses with your group when you meet.

read A Gift of Armor

1 Samuel 18:1-5

By the time David had finished reporting to Saul, Jonathan was deeply impressed with David—an immediate bond was forged between them. He became totally committed to David. From that point on he would be David's number-one advocate and friend.

Saul received David into his own household that day, no more to return to the home of his father.

Jonathan, out of his deep love for David, made a covenant with him. He formalized it with solemn gifts: his own royal robe and weapons—armor, sword, bow, and belt.

Whatever Saul gave David to do, he did it—and did it well. So well that Saul put him in charge of his military operations. Everybody, both the people in general and Saul's servants, approved of and admired David's leadership.

---

first thoughts

like:

dislike:

agree:

disagree:

don't get it:

---

think

- The gift of Jonathan's armor symbolized royalty. When Jonathan gave his armor to David, what was he symbolically giving him? Why was the gift so valuable?
- What is the most valuable gift you have given a friend? Describe how it felt to give the gift.
- Why do you think God created a need in every human for friendship? How might this truth help to explain the role friends and community play in defining purpose?
- Reflecting over recent relationships, what kind of a friend have you been? What can you do to be a better friend?

pray

read Is Jean-Luc Just a Fluke?

From "Married to the Job" by Camerin Courtney[1]

I'm having an affair with Jean-Luc. No, not some beret-wearing, cheese-loving French guy (I wish!). No, I'm talking about Jean-Luc, my laptop computer.

I realize this as I'm sitting here writing this column on said paramour while a perfectly fabulous day awaits just feet outside the coffee shop window beside me. I also realized this when Jean-Luc and I walked through the door and the barrista behind the counter started preparing my drink before I even had a chance to utter my high maintenance half-caf, skim, no-whip hazelnut baccio. Obviously our presence here is nothing new.

The people at the quaint little bistro tables around me are chatting happily, as normal people do on weekend days. A woman just entered with a library book to read. Then there's me, working away. Again. Still.

I can argue that I have a column to write and other freelance projects to complete, that writing is in some ways "home" to me. But when I'm really honest, I admit I've been spending way too much time with Jean-Luc of late. And way too much time at work. I'm usually there until 6:30 p.m., and closing time's 4:30 p.m. I'm becoming a bit of a workaholic.

This is nothing new in our overworked, prove-your-worth-by-how-busy-you-are culture. But when I recently recognized the relationship between my singleness and my workaholism, I knew something needed to change.

I walked out of work around 7 p.m. and realized the only other two cars in the parking lot belonged to fellow single people. Telling, no?

Sure, we have more flexibility to stay late and get things done. And yes, I sometimes get my second wind about ten minutes before quitting time. But, again, when I'm honest, I also admit that sometimes I don't go home as early as I should not because there's so much work to do, but because no one's waiting there for me.

At work I have community and roles to fill; someone notices when I complete a task (or don't!). In contrast, at home I have solitude and purely self-motivation for projects that must be completed. No one notices when I pay the bills or clean my bathroom. My pet parakeet doesn't even chirp his appreciation.

And sometimes, needed downtime in the evenings simply seems lonely. Since I live alone, there's no built-in community when I go home. Company can be hard to come by as everyone else is just as crazy-busy. And in reality, sometimes I don't even want much interaction, just someone else's presence. Even just a friend sitting across the room while we each read our respective novels, or a romantic interest whose lap I can rest my feet in while we silently watch TV together.

Regardless of how much interaction we want with others, or how we want to enjoy or fill our time off, it takes something I often forget: intentionality. Ironi-cally, I was reminded of this recently when I was reeling from a breakup. I was brokenhearted and having a hard time being alone, so I called up just about everyone I know to schedule lunches, dinners, evening coffee runs. Though we were talking through tough emotions part of the time, part of me simply enjoyed the constant community. I had a different sense of peace and con-nectedness that week.

---

first thoughts

like:

dislike:

agree:

disagree:

don't get it:

---

think

- Who or what is the Jean-Luc in your life?
- Who (in addition to God) do you turn to when circumstances in life turn rotten? Why are those people so important?
- Describe a moment when you turned to a community of friends during a time of need. What was the response? What did they

do right? What did they do wrong? How does that affect how
you will respond the next time someone you know is in need?

- What role do you allow your friends and mentors to play in your
personal spiritual growth? In what ways do you inhibit them
from playing a greater role in your growth?

pray

read Friends in High Places

Daniel 2:14-23

When Arioch, chief of the royal guards, was making arrangements for the execution, Daniel wisely took him aside and quietly asked what was going on: "Why this all of a sudden?"

After Arioch filled in the background, Daniel went to the king and asked for a little time so that he could interpret the dream.

Daniel then went home and told his companions Hananiah, Mishael, and Azariah what was going on. He asked them to pray to the God of heaven for mercy in solving this mystery so that the four of them wouldn't be killed along with the whole company of Babylonian wise men.

That night the answer to the mystery was given to Daniel in a vision. Daniel blessed the God of heaven, saying,

"Blessed be the name of God,
      forever and ever.
He knows all, does all:
      He changes the seasons and guides history,
He raises up kings and also brings them down,
      he provides both intelligence and discernment,
He opens up the depths, tells secrets,
      sees in the dark—light spills out of him!
God of all my ancestors, all thanks! all praise!
      You made me wise and strong.
And now you've shown us what we asked for.
      You've solved the king's mystery."

first thoughts

like:

dislike:

agree:

disagree:

don't get it:

think

- How do you think the friendship between Hananiah, Mishael, Azariah, and Daniel helped each of them to remain faithful to God?
- How has God used friends in your own life to strengthen your faith?
- What is the purpose of friends? In what ways is being a friend to others part of your purpose?

pray

read A Vacuum of Friends

From "Are Our Lives Too Busy for Friendship?" by Digby Anderson[2]

How many of your friends do you think will turn up for your funeral?

An elderly priest told me recently: "It is not unusual to conduct a funeral now where no one is present except me and perhaps the deceased's solicitor. The deceased appears to have had no family and no friends. It wasn't always this way."

Or what about this comment from a London GP: "I tell my patients with cancer to think twice before they tell their friends about the nature of their disease. My experience is that on learning of the diagnosis, many so-called friends will cease to visit the sick person." Friendship in Britain today is in trouble.

It was announced earlier this year that schools in England are introducing classes in friendship because children no longer know how to make friends. A society which imagines you can teach friendship is, I believe, a society in crisis.

Friendship is not publicly recorded. No registry office legally establishes it. No church blesses it. So anyone is free to claim they have ten or a hundred friends and no one can say otherwise. But it is this lack of public recognition of friendship which is one of the signs of its decline.

Thousands of books are written about the family, but next to none on friendship.

Modern Britain does not publicly honor friendship. But if we paused to consider who our "friends" are, I think we would find many of our so-called friendships are not true friendships at all.

Young people talk about having made a "new friend" at the weekend. But true friendship takes time to grow. People equate their friends with the fun they have with them, whereas it is the tough times shared which bring friends closer together.

Friendship is failing for many reasons: our increasingly busy and transient lives and more family breakdown. And we are less trusting and more cynical than we used to be.

Paradoxically, we are more sociable than our ancestors.

Through work, travel and socializing we come into contact with many more people than they did. But this works against making real friends. We make acquaintances masquerading as friends.

Friendship is failing, too, because our age is obsessed with making things equal for everyone and achieving it by excessive bureaucracy.

In business, especially, equal opportunities reign. Appoint or promote a friend and you will have the equal opportunities police called in.

Yet business, especially in the City of London, used to be done on trust.

A friend putting money into another friend's business venture launched many of the great banks and businesses in the 19th century.

To trust someone, you need to know them as an acquaintance or friend, or have them vouched for by a mutual friend. We know far more about our friends than about strangers, and that means we know more about their suitability for a job or higher position.

No true friend would take a job for which he or she was unsuited because it would not be right—no one wants a cheat for a friend—and because it would get a friend into trouble.

True friends don't corrupt each other, they keep each other on the straight and narrow.

So friendship is being driven out of work, out of politics, out of the prestigious parts of life. It finds itself confined to recreation, to passing the odd hour together in the pub, club or coffee shop. But even there it is not safe.

first thoughts
like:
dislike:
agree:
disagree:
don't get it:

think

- In what ways have you observed a void of friendships in our society? Is there a particular group of people who tend to be the most overlooked?
- What kind of impact does loneliness have on the human soul? What kind of impact has it had on your soul?
- What risks are associated with authentic community and real relationships? Do you think the benefits outweigh the risks? In what ways?
- What prevents you from going deeper in your friendships and relationships? What holds you back?

pray

read   A Family of Friends

**From *Winging It: Meditations of a Young Adult* by
Therese Johnson Borchard**[3]

"Do these jeans make me look fat?" I ask my sister as I zip up a new pair of
Calvin Klein denims and look in the bathroom mirror.

"No," she replies. "Your butt makes you look fat."

Only a sister—and only one I'm getting along with at the time—can get
away with a crack like this. It's true what they say, that blood is thicker than
water.

I've been blessed with three sisters, although in high school it felt more like
a curse. One lost my favorite sweater, the other my fake ID, while the third was
busy flirting with my heartthrob. As four sisters born within four years of each
other, we competed for everything, especially the attention of our parents. Like
puppies born of the same litter, we growled and wrestled with each other to
determine our place in the family. But it made us stronger, healthier and much
better at sharing.

Now we're friends, and closer than ever, although we have never grown out of the roles we staked out early on. My older sister is the responsible one, the golden child; my twin sister, the impulsive one, who dislikes all kinds of rules. And the middle sister and I, we are peacemakers, or the superglue that holds everything together (oftentimes unnaturally), extinguishing fires as soon as they ignite.

I have become the counselor and therefore receive the depressed calls. The second oldest is the entertainer and is responsible

first thoughts

like:

dislike:

agree:

disagree:

don't get it:

for laughs. My twin adds an element of spontaneity to our lives, as she never tires of random adventures. And the oldest plans family reunions and offers us helpful investment tips.

It's chaos at times, especially when you introduce boyfriends and husbands into the fold. Feelings get hurt, insecurities emerge—you know, the recipe for a dysfunctional family. Yet, in all of it, we have grown to love, appreciate and support each other, which is why we can say the things that we do.

think

- How are your relationships with family members different from your relationships with friends?
- How do your relationships with particular family members strengthen and encourage you as an individual? How do they prove challenging?
- Why do you think God created the family?
- What can you do to deepen your relationships with your family?
- How can family relationships help to define you and your purpose?

pray

live   The Redefining

Take a few moments to skim through the notes you've made in these readings. What do they tell you about your connection with true community? Based on what you've read and discussed, is there anything you want to change? Describe this below.

What, if anything, is stopping you from making this change?

Reflect on your circle of friends for a few moments. Does the group have any healthy habits that need to be reinforced? Does the group have any unhealthy habits that need to be changed? How can you encourage your friends to live a God-infused life?

God has placed you in a family. As you reflect over the last year, can you think of examples of how God has used your family members to both challenge and encourage you? What steps can you take to be a better friend to your family members?

Talk with a close friend about all of the above. Brainstorm together about what it might take to move toward God in this area of your life. Determine what this looks like in a practical sense and then list any measurable goals you want to shoot for here. Review these goals each week to see how you're doing.

that church
connection

All this energy issues from Christ: God raised him from death and set him on a throne in deep heaven, in charge of running the universe, everything from galaxies to governments, no name and no power exempt from his rule. And not just for the time being, but *forever*. He is in charge of it all, has the final word on everything. At the center of all this, Christ rules the church. The church, you see, is not peripheral to the world; the world is peripheral to the church. The church is Christ's body, in which he speaks and acts, by which he fills everything with his presence.

Ephesians 1:20-23

a reminder

Before you dive into this study, spend a little time reviewing what you wrote in the previous lessons' Live sections. How are you doing? Check with your small-group members and review your progress toward the specified goals. If necessary, adjust your goals and plans and then recommit to them.

the defining line

God could choose to manifest Himself through anything, yet He chose the church—the body of Christ—to reveal Himself to the world. Clearly, God created the church for some amazing purpose.

redefininglife

How do you define *church*? What does the church look like? What do you think it should look like?

If you are a follower of Jesus, then you are part of the body of Christ. What is your function within the body? How are you fulfilling that function? Explore these questions in the space below.

Consider sharing your responses with your group when you meet.

read Here's the Church

From *The Ball and the Cross* by G. K. Chesterton[1]

When we belong to the Church we belong to something which is outside all of us; which is outside everything you talk about, outside the Cardinals and the Pope. They belong to it, but it does not belong to them. If we all fell dead suddenly, the Church would somehow exist in God.

From *Leaves from the Notebook of a Tamed Cynic* by Reinhold Niebuhr[2]

What we accomplish in the way of church unity ought to be accepted with humility and not hailed with pride. We are not creating. We are merely catching up with creation.

---

first thoughts

like:

dislike:

agree:

disagree:

don't get it:

---

think

- What is the church to you? Is what you believe about the church today any different than what you believed as a child? Explain the differences.
- What is your reaction to Chesterton's statement that "the Church would somehow exist in God"?
- How are we "catching up with creation" in the church?
- What are your greatest disappointments regarding the church? In what ways has the church surprised you in a positive way?
- How would you describe your church?

pray

read Leftover Body Parts

James 2:1-7

My dear friends, don't let public opinion influence how you live out our glorious, Christ-originated faith. If a man enters your church wearing an expensive suit, and a street person wearing rags comes in right after him, and you say to the man in the suit, "Sit here, sir; this is the best seat in the house!" and either ignore the street person or say, "Better sit here in the back row," haven't you segregated God's children and proved that you are judges who can't be trusted?

Listen, dear friends. Isn't it clear by now that God operates quite differently? He chose the world's down-and-out as the kingdom's first citizens, with full rights and privileges. This kingdom is promised to anyone who loves God. And here you are abusing these same citizens! Isn't it the high and mighty who exploit you, who use the courts to rob you blind? Aren't they the ones who scorn the new name—"Christian"—used in your baptisms?

---

first thoughts

like:

dislike:

agree:

disagree:

don't get it:

---

think

- In what ways have you shown a prejudice toward different types of Christians? What does this reveal about your heart and motives?
- How does judging other Christians affect the body of Christ? When does it strengthen it? When does it impede it?
- In what ways do you consciously recognize the kingdom of God in your own life?
- What role does church play in your life purpose? What role should it play?

pray

read Embracing the Body

Hebrews 10:19-25

So, friends, we can now—without hesitation—walk right up to God, into "the Holy Place." Jesus has cleared the way by the blood of his sacrifice, acting as our priest before God. The "curtain" into God's presence is his body.

So let's *do* it—full of belief, confident that we're presentable inside and out. Let's keep a firm grip on the promises that keep us going. He always keeps his word. Let's see how inventive we can be in encouraging love and helping out, not avoiding worshiping together as some do but spurring each other on, especially as we see the big Day approaching.

---

first thoughts

like:

dislike:

agree:

disagree:

don't get it:

---

think

- What is the link between experiencing community—experiencing what church is meant to be—and not losing faith?
- Why do you think God created a community of believers (the church)?

- Describe a moment in your life when you saw a community of believers acting as a true body. What did it look like? What was the impact on others? How did it impact you?

pray

read The Walking Wounded

From "The Church's Walking Wounded: How Should We Respond in a Psychological Age?" by Tim Stafford[3]

I received a letter from an old friend, a pastor's wife. She used shaded and painstaking words, language intended to convey deep personal struggle without giving too much in the way of detail. To this day I don't know exactly what happened to her and who ultimately was at fault—if anyone. Nevertheless, the tone of her letter made miserably clear that she was wounded.

Not, apparently, wounded by any single person or event but—as she saw it—wounded by the church. After a lifetime of engagement, she has dropped out of active involvement. She indicated she needed to learn how to experience Jesus' love instead of guilt and duty.

This friend had sought help. Philip Yancey's writings have meant a great deal to her. A therapist has provided support and insight, helping her learn to care for herself. As if to allay any misunderstandings, she wrote that her husband had been supportive and understanding.

But when she would be back in circulation, she could not say.

I read the letter with a sinking feeling, not just from pity for my friend, but also because she reminded me of an epidemic I have been uneasily witnessing. Every time I turn around, I meet another person like her, who feels wounded by the church.

Of course, churches are human institutions, and they have been disappointing people since the time of Peter. I doubt, though, that this has ever translated so readily into individuals who carry

first thoughts

like:

dislike:

agree:

disagree:

don't get it:

around their pain, who suffer emotionally and spiritually so deeply that they are virtually disabled. I think we have more such people about than ever before—many more. . . .

People may be wounded by the world, but when they come to church, they hope for better treatment. If they perceive that the church has not treated them as they hoped it would, the pain may be intense.

think

- The church doesn't always respond to people in a manner reflective of Christ. Have you ever been wounded by fellow believers? If so, what was important or helpful on the path to recovery and healing?
- Even with its imperfections, God still uses the modern-day church. Why do you think God uses an imperfect institution to reflect Himself to the world?
- Is it important to attend church regularly? Why or why not?
- Do you have a specific role in your local church (other than "weekly chair warmer")? Do you look forward to participating in that role, or do you avoid it? Explain.

pray

read The Panorama of God

From *Authentic Relationships: Discover the Lost Art of "One Anothering"* by Wayne Jacobsen and Clay Jacobsen[4]

I gazed out the window at the snow-covered hills that surrounded the New England retreat. I had accompanied my brother to the retreat to help lead worship. I was not prepared for the revelation the Spirit would birth in my heart that day. Wayne was speaking on the power of Christian friendship focusing on Scriptures he called the "one anothering" passages.

At first blush his message didn't seem to be anything new. I had been raised by loving, Christian parents and had read these verses individually dozens of times. Though many of them were some of the most enduring passages I had studied in the course of my life, I had never considered them together in this context. Combined, they painted a rich panorama of the incredible relationships of love and support that the Body of Christ can share.

My retreat experience was a powerful, life-changing moment in my walk with the Lord. As I began to grasp the lost art of one-anothering, I started on a journey that has redefined how I view the church, how I relate to other Christians, and even how I relate to God. It has also helped me cultivate better friendships with other believers and people in the world who do not yet know God.

first thoughts
like:
dislike:
agree:
disagree:
don't get it:

think

- What do you think this "one anothering" is that this article talks about? Do you see evidence of it in your church and in your life? What role does this kind of living play in defining your purpose?
- Are the majority of your friends followers of Jesus or non-believers? What steps have you taken to cultivate better friend-ships with other believers? What steps have you taken to cultivate friendships with nonbelievers?
- In what ways are your friendships with followers of Jesus different from those with nonbelievers? With whom can you share more of your true self?
- If the modern church didn't have any imperfections, what would it look like? What are you doing to help make that a reality?

pray

live   The Redefining

Take a few moments to skim through the notes you've made in these readings. What do they tell you about how you relate to the church? Based on what you've read and discussed, is there anything you want to change? Describe this below.

What, if anything, is stopping you from making this change?

What attitudes toward the church, if any, do you need to change? What can you do to help make the church what it's supposed to be?

If God designed the church as a community of believers, how do you fit into this community? What is your role? How can you embrace that role?

Talk with a close friend about all of the above. Brainstorm together about what it might take to move toward God in this area of your life. Determine what this looks like in a practical sense and then list any measurable goals you want to shoot for here. Review these goals each week to see how you're doing.

the greater
good

"This is the kind of fast day I'm after:
      to break the chains of injustice,
      get rid of exploitation in the workplace,
      free the oppressed,
      cancel debts.
What I'm interested in seeing you do is:
      sharing your food with the hungry,
      inviting the homeless poor into your homes,
      putting clothes on the shivering ill-clad,
      being available to your own families."

                                    Isaiah 58:6-7

a reminder

Before you dive into this study, spend a little time reviewing what you wrote in the previous lessons' Live sections. How are you doing? Check with your small-group members and review your progress toward the specified goals. If necessary, adjust your goals and plans and then recommit to them.

the defining line

God cares more about breaking oppression than religious fasts and works that look good on the outside. His desire is that we serve others and in the process reflect Him. Yep, it's another piece of the greater purpose. Followers of Christ are invited to take part in works of social justice, evangelism, and missions—whether or not they leave their native soil.

In what ways do you see injustice in your own city? Where do you see injustice at work? How about in your neighborhood?

Do you feel compelled to respond to these injustices? Why or why not?

What about the call to reach out to others with the good news? Do you feel that? What do you do about it?

Consider sharing your responses with your group when you meet.

read Get Help from God

Psalm 146

Hallelujah!
　　O my soul, praise GOD!
All my life long I'll praise GOD,
　　singing songs to my God as long as I live.

Don't put your life in the hands of experts
　　who know nothing of life, of *salvation* life.
Mere humans don't have what it takes;
　　when they die, their projects die with them.
Instead, get help from the God of Jacob,
　　put your hope in GOD and know real blessing!
GOD made sky and soil,
　　sea and all the fish in it.
He always does what he says—
　　he defends the wronged,
　　he feeds the hungry.
GOD frees prisoners—
　　he gives sight to the blind,
　　he lifts up the fallen,
GOD loves good people, protects strangers,
　　takes the side of orphans and widows,
　　but makes short work of the wicked.

GOD's in charge—*always.*
　　Zion's God is God for good!
Hallelujah!

first thoughts

like:

dislike:

agree:

disagree:

don't get it:

think

- How is God's concern for the poor reflected in your life?
- In what ways have you had the opportunity to defend the wronged, feed the hungry, protect strangers, and help orphans and widows?
- How is serving these people fulfilling God's purpose for your life?
- Does this passage inspire you to adjust your current priorities? Why or why not?

pray

read The Return of the King

Matthew 25:31-46

"When he finally arrives, blazing in beauty and all his angels with him, the Son of Man will take his place on his glorious throne. Then all the nations will be arranged before him and he will sort the people out, much as a shepherd sorts out sheep and goats, putting sheep to his right and goats to his left.

"Then the King will say to those on his right, 'Enter, you who are blessed by my Father! Take what's coming to you in this kingdom. It's been ready for you since the world's foundation. And here's why:

> I was hungry and you fed me,
> I was thirsty and you gave me a drink,
> I was homeless and you gave me a room,
> I was shivering and you gave me clothes,
> I was sick and you stopped to visit,
> I was in prison and you came to me.'

"Then those 'sheep' are going to say, 'Master, what are you talking about? When did we ever see you hungry and feed you, thirsty and give you a drink? And when did we ever see you sick or in prison and come to you?' Then the King will say, 'I'm telling the solemn truth: Whenever you did one of these things to someone overlooked or ignored, that was me—you did it to me.'

"Then he will turn to the 'goats,' the ones on his left, and say, 'Get out, worthless goats! You're good for nothing but the fires of hell. And why? Because—

> I was hungry and you gave me no meal,
> I was thirsty and you gave me no drink,
> I was homeless and you gave me no bed,
> I was shivering and you gave me no clothes,
> Sick and in prison, and you never visited.'

"Then those 'goats' are going to say, 'Master, what are you talking about? When did we ever see you hungry or thirsty or homeless or shivering or sick or in prison and didn't help?'

"He will answer them, 'I'm telling the solemn truth: Whenever you failed to do one of these things to someone who was being overlooked or ignored, that was me—you failed to do it to me.'

first thoughts

like:

dislike:

agree:

disagree:

don't get it:

"Then those 'goats' will be herded to their eternal doom, but the 'sheep' to their eternal reward."

think

- Why do you think God places such a high importance on caring for the needy?
- Do you think there's a link between caring for people and living a life of obedience to Christ? Explain.
- Can you think of anyone you have overlooked or ignored? What made you turn away? What would help you to turn back and reach out with help?
- Why does it often seem easy to justify doing nothing at all?
- If your purpose is tied into the person God created you to be, are you fighting your purpose if you don't reach out to people in need? Explain.

pray

read Surprising Generosity

Romans 12:16-21

Get along with each other; don't be stuck-up. Make friends with nobodies; don't be the great somebody.

Don't hit back; discover beauty in everyone. If you've got it in you, get along with everybody. Don't insist on getting even; that's not for you to do. "I'll do the judging," says God. "I'll take care of it."

Our Scriptures tell us that if you see your enemy hungry, go buy that person lunch, or if he's thirsty, get him a drink. Your generosity will surprise him with goodness. Don't let evil get the best of you; get the best of evil by doing good.

---

first thoughts

like:

dislike:

agree:

disagree:

don't get it:

---

think

- Why does God command such generosity from us?
- Does this sort of lifestyle seem impossible? Unrealistic? A great goal? How does this passage affect the way you see God's purpose for you?

- How do you discover beauty in people? When was the last time you discovered beauty in someone? What helped you to see the beauty?
- When have you allowed evil to get the best of you? When have you been able to get the best of evil by doing good?

pray

read Eyes Wide Open

From "How Few There Are Who Die So Hard" by John Piper[1]

Patrick Johnstone says in *Operation World* that only in the 1990s did we get a reasonably complete listing of the world's peoples. For the first time we can see clearly what is left to be done. There are about 12,000 ethnolinguistic peoples in the world. About 3,500 of these have, on average, 1.2% Christian populations—about 20 million of the 1.7 billion people, using the broadest, nominal definition of Christian. Most of these least reached 3,500 peoples are in the 10/40 window and are religiously unsympathetic to Christian missions. That means that that we must go to these peoples with the gospel, and it will be dangerous and costly. Some of us and some of our children will be killed.

When Adoniram Judson entered Burma in July, 1813 it was a hostile and utterly unreached place. William Carey had told Judson in India a few months earlier not to go there. It probably would have been considered a closed country today—with anarchic despotism, fierce war with Siam, enemy raids, constant rebellion, no religious toleration. All the previous missionaries had died or left.

But Judson went there with his 23-year-old wife of 17 months. He was 24 years old and he worked there for 38 years until his death at age 61, with one trip home to New England after 33 years. The price he paid was immense. He was a seed that fell into the ground and died. And the fruit God gave is celebrated even in scholarly works like David Barrett's *World Christian Encyclopedia*: "The largest Christian force in Burma is the Burma Baptist Convention, which owes its origin to the pioneering activity of the American Baptist missionary Adoniram Judson."

Judson was a Baptist when he entered Burma in 1813, even though he left New England as a Congregationalist. His mind had changed during the 114-day voyage to India and Carey's colleague, William Ward, baptized Adoniram and Ann Judson in India on September 6, 1812. Today Patrick Johnstone estimates the Myanmar (Burma's new name) Baptist Convention to be 3,700 congregations with 617,781 members and 1,900,000 affiliates—the fruit of this dead seed.

Of course there were others besides Adoniram Judson—hundreds of others over time. But they too came and gave away their lives. Most of them died much younger than Judson. They only serve to make the point. The astonishing fruit in Myanmar today has grown in the soil of the suffering and death of many missionaries, especially Adoniram Judson.

My question is, if Christ delays his return another two hundred years—a mere fraction of a day in his reckoning—which of you will have suffered and died so that the triumphs of grace will be told about one or two of those 3,500 peoples who are in the same condition today that the Karen and Chin and Kachins and Burmese were in 1813? Who will labor so long and so hard and so perseveringly that in two hundred years there will be two million Christians in many of the 10/40-window peoples who can scarcely recall their Muslim or Hindu or Buddhist roots?

---

first thoughts

like:

dislike:

agree:

disagree:

don't get it:

---

think

- Have you ever felt prompted to do mission work, whether locally or internationally? How did you respond?
- Is mission-mindedness critical to those who seek God's purpose for their lives? Or can you find purpose without any sense of missional living?
- Can you live a missional life if you never leave your native country? If so, how?
- What changes do you need to make to be more missions minded?

pray

read A Mission-Infused Life

From *Winging It: Meditations of a Young Adult* by Therese Johnson Borchard[2]

A few months back I had lunch with a priest friend in the entertainment business. I asked him if he ever feels like a fish out of water—a man of the cloth representing the church of God in the middle of Hollywood. His response surprised me and has been food for thought ever since.

"You can't be a missionary," he said, "unless you're on the other guy's turf."

I didn't initially think of him as a missionary. But, until he said that, I didn't consider myself one either, nor the countless other people spreading the word of God in nontraditional ways, like the guy you see on nationally televised basketball games holding up the John 3:16 poster (who somehow manages to get front billing each game).

If a missionary is any person whose work is to point others to the love of God and to the hope of the Gospel message, then poster boy, Fr. Hollywood, and I are all missionaries. . . .

My priest encourages screenwriters and filmmakers to proceed with integrity and to develop products that inspire goodness—his challenge as well. And I try to share the good news in the books I write and in the talks I give around the country, as well as passing on love and hope at the places I frequent on a

first thoughts
like:
dislike:
agree:
disagree:
don't get it:

regular basis—the coffee shop, the gym, the grocery store.

In our own ways, we have all gone to the other guy's turf to be a missionary.

think

- How do you respond to the claim that "you can't be a missionary unless you're on the other guy's turf"?
- Where is "the other guy's turf" for you?
- Do you make an active choice to fulfill Jesus' command to preach and teach the gospel—to fulfill what many call the Great Commission?
- In what ways do you embrace the idea of telling others about Jesus? In what ways do you shrink away from it?
- Redefine *missionary* based on your thoughts in this chapter (and any discussion you've had with friends about this).
- Using your revised definition, answer the following question: Is being some kind of missionary essential to living out God's purpose for you? What kind of missionary do you feel drawn to be?

pray

live The Redefining

Take a few moments to skim through the notes you've made in these readings. What do they tell you about how a missional approach to life fits in with your life purpose? Based on what you've read and discussed, is there anything you want to change? Describe this below.

What, if anything, is stopping you from making this change?

Review the rough draft statement of your purpose from the end of the first section. What would you add? What would you change? How would you personalize the statement? Record your new version below.

What practical steps do you need to take to live out the mission statement you just created? Make a list below. Ask group members to hold you accountable to these steps (meet periodically to talk about how you're doing).

And don't stop here. Even though you've come to the end of this study, this is only the beginning of the redefining process. It will last a lifetime. Yet by examining these many different areas of your faith life, you've begun an internal (and eternal) dialogue about purpose, about significance, about *why you are here*. Reflect on what you've uncovered and don't be afraid to keep wrestling with the things you don't quite understand. Come back to this book often to remind yourself of the big goals you've set and the specific ideas you have for reaching them. And take a moment to pray as well, asking God to congeal some of these thoughts into wisdom that will inform the rest of your life.

discussion group
study tips

After going through the study on your own, it's time to sit down with others and go deeper. A group of eight to ten is optimal, but smaller groups will allow members to participate more.

Here are a few thoughts on how to make the most of your group discussion time.

Set ground rules. You don't need many. Here are two:

First, you'll want group members to make a commitment to the entire eight-week study. A binding legal document with notarized signatures and commitments written in blood probably isn't necessary—but *you* know your friends best. Just remember this: Significant personal growth happens when group members spend enough time together to really get to know each other. Hit-and-miss attendance rarely allows this to occur.

Second, agree together that everyone's story is important. Time is a valuable commodity, so if you have only an hour to spend together, do your best to give each person ample time to express concerns, pass along insights, and generally feel like a participating member of the group. Small-group discussions are not monologues.

Meet regularly. Choose a time and place and stick to it. No one likes showing up to a restaurant at noon, only to discover that the meeting was moved to seven in the evening at so-and-so's house. Consistency removes stress that could otherwise frustrate discussion and subsequent personal growth. It's only eight weeks. You can do this.

Think ahead. Whoever is leading or organizing the study needs to keep an eye on the calendar. No matter what day or time you pick, you're probably going to run into a date that just doesn't work for people. Maybe it's a holiday. Maybe there's a huge concert or conference in town. Maybe there's a random week when everyone is going to be out of town. Keep in communication with each other about the meetings and be flexible if you do have to reschedule a meeting or skip a week.

Talk openly. If you enter this study with shields up, you're probably not alone. And you're not a "bad person" for your hesitation to unpack your life in front of friends or strangers. Maybe you're skeptical about the value of revealing the deepest parts of who you are to others. Maybe you're simply too afraid of what might fall out of the suitcase. You don't have to go to a place where you're uncomfortable. If you want to sit and listen, offer a few thoughts, or even express a surface level of your own pain, go ahead. But don't neglect what brings you to this place—that desperation. You can't ignore it away. Dip your feet in the water of brutally honest discussion and you may choose to dive in. There is healing here.

Stay on task. Be wary of sharing material that falls into the Too Much Information (TMI) category. Don't spill unnecessary stuff. This is about discovering how *you* can be a better person.

Hold each other accountable. The Live section is an important gear in the "redefinition" machine. If you're really ready for positive change—for spiritual growth—you'll want to take this section seriously. Get personal when you summarize your discoveries. Be practical as you compose your goals. And make sure you're realistic as you determine a plan for accountability. Be extraordinarily loving but brutally honest as you examine each other's Live sections. The stuff on this page must be doable. Don't hold back—this is where the rubber meets the road.

frequently asked questions

I'm stuck. I've read the words on the page, but they just don't connect. Am I missing something?

Be patient. There's no need for speed-reading. Reread the words. Pray about them. Reflect on the questions at the bottom of the page. Consider rewriting the reading in a way that makes sense to you. Meditate on one idea at a time. Read Scripture passages in different Bible translations. Ask a friend for help. Skip the section and come back to it later. And don't beat yourself up if you still don't connect. Turn the page and keep seeking.

This study includes a wide variety of readings. Some are intended to provoke. Others are intended to subdue. Some are meant to apply to a thinker, others to a feeler, and still others to an experiential learner. If your groove is pop culture, science, relationships, art, or something completely different, there's something in here that you're naturally going to click with, but that doesn't mean that you should just brush off the rest of the readings. It means that in those no-instant-click moments, you're going to have to broaden your perspective and think outside your own box. You may be surprised by what you discover.

One or two people in our small group tend to dominate the discussion. Is there any polite way of handling this?

Did you set up ground rules with your group? If not, review the suggestions above and incorporate them. Then do this: Before each discussion, remind participants that each person's thoughts, insights, concerns, and opinions are important. Note the time you have for your meeting and then dive in.

If this still doesn't help, you may need to speak to the person who has arm-wrestled control. Do so in a loving manner, expressing your sincere concern for what the person is talking about and inviting others to weigh in as well. Please note: A one-person-dominated discussion isn't *always* a bad thing. Your role in a small group is not only to explore and expand your own understanding; it's also to support one another. If someone truly needs more of the floor, give it to him. There will be times when the needs of the one outweigh the needs of the many. Use good judgment and allow extra space when needed. Your time might be next week.

One or two people in our small group rarely say anything. How should we handle this?

Recognize that not everyone will be comfortable sharing. Depending on her background, personality, and comfort level, an individual may rarely say anything at all. There are two things to remember. First, love a person right where she is. This may be one of her first experiences as part of a Bible discussion group. She may be feeling insecure because she doesn't know the Bible as well as other members of the group. She may just be shy or introverted. She may still be sorting out what she believes. Whatever the case, make her feel welcome and loved. Thank her for coming, and if she misses a meeting, call to check up on her. After one of the studies, you may want to ask her what she thought about the discussion. And after a few meetings, you can try to involve her in the discussion by asking everyone in the group to respond to a certain question. Just make sure the question you ask doesn't put anyone on the spot.

During our meeting time, we find ourselves spending so much time catching up with each other — what happened over the previous week — that we don't have enough time for the actual study.

If the friendships within your group grow tight, you may need to establish some time just to hang out and catch up with one another. This is a healthy part of a successful discussion group. You can do this before or after the actual study group time. Some groups prefer to share a meal together before the study, and other groups prefer to stay afterward and munch on snacks.

Whatever your group chooses, it's important to have established start and finish times for your group members. That way, the people who are on a tight schedule can know when to show up to catch the main part of the meeting.

At our meetings, there are times when one or two people will become really vulnerable about something they're struggling with or facing. It's an awkward thing for our group to try to handle. What should we do?

This study is designed to encourage group members to get real and be vulnerable. But how your group deals with those vulnerabilities will determine how much deeper your group can go. If a person is sharing something that makes him particularly vulnerable, avoid offering a quick, fix-it answer. Even if you know how to heal deep hurts, cure eating disorders, or overcome depression in one quick answer, hold your tongue. Most people who make themselves vulnerable aren't looking for a quick fix. They want two things: to know they aren't alone and to be supported. If you can identify with their hurt, say so, without one-upping their story with your own. Second, let the person know you'll pray for him, and if the moment is right, go ahead and pray for him right then. If the moment isn't right, then you may want to pray for him at the end of the meeting. Walking through these vulnerable times is tricky business, and it's going to take a lot of prayer and listening to God's leading to get you through.

Some group members don't prepare before our meetings. How can we encourage them to read ahead of time?

It can be frustrating, particularly as a leader, when group members don't read the material; but don't let this discourage you. You can begin each lesson by reading the section together as a group so that everyone is on the same page. And you can gently encourage group members to read during the week. But ultimately, what really matters is that they show up and are growing spiritually alongside you. The REDEFINING LIFE studies aren't about homework; they're about personal spiritual growth, and that takes place in many ways—both inside and outside this book. So if someone's slacking on the outside, it's okay. You have no idea how much she may be growing or being challenged on the inside.

Our group members are having a tough time reaching their goals. What can we do?

First of all, review the goals you've set. Are they realistic? How would you measure a goal of "don't be frustrated at work"? Rewrite the goals until they're bite-sized and reasonable—and reachable. How about "Take an online personality test" or "Make a list of what's good and what's not-so-good about my career choices so I can talk about it with discussion group members" or "Start keeping a prayer journal." Get practical. Get real. And don't forget to marinate everything in lots of prayer.

notes

Lesson 1

1. Myles Werntz, "Finding Yourself in 'Love,'" *Relevant*, n.d., http://www. relevantmagazine.com/article.php?sid=3769.
2. JoAnna Harris, *You Didn't Complete Me: When "the One" Turns Out to Be Just Someone* (Nashville: W Publishing Group, 2004).

Lesson 2

1. "Grace," *Blessings for Life*, http://blessingsforlife.com/favforwards/ gracestudent.htm.

Lesson 3

1. Joni Eareckson Tada, "Joni Eareckson: Victory Through Suffering," *Power to Change*, n.d., http://www.powertochange.com/changed/jeareckson.html.
2. Margaret Feinberg, *God Whispers: Learning to Hear His Voice* (Lake Mary, Fla.: Relevant Books, 2002), p. 21.

Lesson 4

1. David Crowder, *Praise Habit: Finding God in Sunsets and Sushi* (Colorado Springs, Colo.: TH1NK, 2005), pp. 20-21.
2. Matt Redman, "Tim Hughes Interview," *Heart of Worship*, August 1, 2004, http://www.heartofworship.com/features/index.php?page=archive.

Lesson 5

1. G. K. Chesterton, *Orthodoxy* in *Nelson's Royal Classics: Heretics/Orthodoxy* (Nashville: Nelson, 2000), pp. 273-274.
2. "Happiness: Seize the Moment Finding Copper Pennies," *christianity.com*, September 24, 2004, http://forums.christianity.com/html/P1157912/.

Lesson 6

1. Camerin Courtney, "Married to the Job," *ChristianityToday.com*, August 25, 2004, http://www.christianitytoday.com/singles/newsletter/mind40825.html.
2. Digby Anderson, "Are Our Lives Too Busy for Friendship?" *The Daily Mail* (London), November 12, 2001.
3. Therese Johnson Borchard, *Winging It: Meditations of a Young Adult* (Maryknoll, N.Y.: Orbis Books, 2001), pp. 46-47.

Lesson 7

1. G. K. Chesterton, *The Ball and the Cross* (Mancola, N.Y.: Dover Publications, 1995).
2. Reinhold Niebuhr, *Leaves from the Notebook of a Tamed Cynic*, reissue ed. (Louisville, Ky.: Westminster John Knox Press, 1991).
3. Tim Stafford, "The Church's Walking Wounded: How Should We Respond in a Psychological Age?" *Christianity Today*, March 2003, p. 64.
4. Wayne Jacobsen and Clay Jacobsen, *Authentic Relationships: Discover the Lost Art of "One Anothering"* (Grand Rapids, Mich.: Baker, 2003), http://www.lifestream.org/LSauthentic1.html.

Lesson 8

1. John Piper, "How Few There Are Who Die So Hard," *Desiring God*, February 4, 2003, http://www.desiringgod.org/library/biographies/03judson.html.
2. Therese Johnson Borchard, *Winging It: Meditations of a Young Adult* (Maryknoll, N.Y.: Orbis Books, 2001), pp. 134-135.

OWN YOUR FAITH.

Redefining Life: My Identity

Who are you?
Who are you when no one is watching?
Who are you when it's just you alone in a room with God?
These are tough questions—the kind that cut to the core of
our beings. They strip us of our titles, background, ethnicity,
family name, and possessions (or lack thereof). So who are
you? Only you can know. And part of the journey of self-
discovery is God-discovery because He's the One who fashioned you. There is freedom in knowing who you are, and
this discussion guide will help with the process. You'll not only discover what you
were created for but also learn about the One who created you.

TH1NK   1-57683-828-5

The Message//REMIX™

God's Word was meant to be read. But more than that, it was
meant to be understood. It was first written in the language
of the people—of fishermen, shopkeepers, and carpenters.
The Message//REMIX gets back to that: You can read it and
understand it.

In *The Message//REMIX*, verse-numbered paragraphs will
help you study and find favorite passages. Or you can just
read it like a book and let the narrative speak to you. After
all, it is God's story—with heroes and villains, conflicts and
resolutions. It's God's Word—the Truth—in a user-friendly form.

Eugene H. Peterson   1-57683-434-4